JOSSEY-BASS TEACHER

Jossey-Bass Teacher provides educators with practical knowledge and tools to create a positive and lifelong impact on student learning. We offer classroom-tested and research-based teaching resources for a variety of grade levels and subject areas. Whether you are an aspiring, new, or veteran teacher, we want to help you make every teaching day your best.

From ready-to-use classroom activities to the latest teaching framework, our value-packed books provide insightful, practical, and comprehensive materials on the topics that matter most to K–12 teachers. We hope to become your trusted source for the best ideas from the most experienced and respected experts in the field.

JB JOSSEY-BASS™
A Wiley Brand

THE TRANSPARENT TEACHER

Taking Charge of Your Instruction with Peer-Collected Classroom Data

Trent E. Kaufman
Emily Dolci Grimm

Foreword by
Sarah Brown Wessling
2010 National Teacher of the Year

WILEY

Published by Jossey-Bass
A Wiley Imprint
One Montgomery Street, Suite 1200, San Francisco, CA 94104-4594   www.josseybass.com

Jossey-Bass books and products are available through most bookstores. To contact Jossey-Bass directly call our Customer Care Department within the U.S. at 800-956-7739, outside the U.S. at 317-572-3986, or fax 317-572-4002.

Wiley publishes in a variety of print and electronic formats and by print-on-demand. Some material included with standard print versions of this book may not be included in e-books or in print-on-demand. If this book refers to media such as a CD or DVD that is not included in the version you purchased, you may download this material at http://booksupport.wiley.com. For more information about Wiley products, visit www.wiley.com.

Library of Congress Cataloging-in-Publication Data

ISBN 978-1-118-48717-4 (paperback)
ISBN 978-1-118-53921-7 (ebk.)
ISBN 978-1-118-53931-6 (ebk.)
ISBN 978-1-118-53932-3 (ebk.)

Printed in the United States of America
FIRST EDITION
PB Printing 10 9 8 7 6 5 4 3 2 1

ABOUT THE AUTHORS

Trent E. Kaufman is a principal at Education Direction, a school reform research and consultancy firm focused on improving student outcomes across school systems. Education Direction serves state offices of education, school districts, and schools in implementing teacher-driven observation and other data-driven improvement processes. Prior to founding Education Direction, Kaufman served as a teacher, department chair, technology coordinator, athletics coach, dean of students, assistant principal, and principal in northern California. He also previously served as a research and teaching fellow for the Harvard Graduate School of Education, a summer fellow for Industry Initiatives in Science and Math Education, a national faculty member for High School Futures, and a senior analyst for Education Resource Strategies.

Kaufman earned his doctorate in education policy, leadership, and instructional practice from the Harvard Graduate School of Education and his master's degree in education leadership from the University of California at Berkeley. He is the coauthor with Emily Dolci Grimm of *Collaborative School Improvement: Eight Practices for District-School Partnerships to Transform Teaching and Learning* (2012) and the author of a chapter in *Data Wise in Action* (edited by Kathryn Parker Boudett and Jennifer L. Steele, 2007), and his work has been published in *Education Week*.

Kaufman has presented at dozens of conferences, including ASCD's annual conference, Learning Forward, National School Board Association, California League of Schools, Brown University's School Leadership Institute, and the California Charter School Association.

Emily Dolci Grimm has worked as a teacher in both traditional and alternative settings for over a decade. She currently works as a principal at Education Direction. Prior to this position, she served as a teacher, coach, and response to intervention team member at a high school in Maine. While there, she secured grant funding to create and implement the Girls' Aspirations Program, an alternative education program to meet the needs of at-risk girls in the community.

Grimm earned her bachelor's degree from Haverford College and is working toward her master's degree in educational leadership at St. Joseph's College in Standish, Maine. She is the coauthor with Trent E. Kaufman of *Collaborative School Improvement: Eight Practices for District-School Partnerships to Transform Teaching and Learning* (2012), and her work has been published in *Education Week*. She has presented at several conferences, including ASCD's annual conference, Advancing Improvement in Education, and the annual New England League of Middle Schools conference.

ACKNOWLEDGMENTS

Like the teachers and school leaders profiled in this book, time is a resource consistently in short supply for us. We are indebted to our colleagues at Education Direction for their time and for giving us the time to develop and refine this project.

This book has been constructed from the experiences of teachers and school leaders who work tirelessly for the students they serve. Their dedication, persistence, and willingness to open up their practice have built teacher-driven observation into a practice for professional learning. In particular, the educators in the Chandler Unified School District in Chandler, Arizona, and Evansville Vanderburgh School Corporation in Evansville, Indiana, have informed our thinking and illustrated the power of taking charge and opening up their classroom doors.

Fred DePrez, principal at Hamilton High School in Chandler, Arizona, deserves special recognition for his vision and commitment to this work. Our partnership with him has proven invaluable in refining teacher-driven observation. The teachers at Hamilton High have put this vision into action. Patricia Berg, Andrew Burkhart, Phyllis Carr, Shelley Ceinaturaga, and Heather Love, among many other teachers at Hamilton High, have contributed to our understanding of teacher-driven observation in practice. We sincerely thank these pioneers.

We did not write this book alone. Dimi Berkner, Lesley Iura, Linda Manuel, and Marjorie McAneny at Jossey-Bass were instrumental in supporting this project. Two blind reviewers provided valuable feedback that informed its development. Cami Hewett, a talented independent editor, invested countless hours into refining our prose. Our colleague Allison Miller provided valuable feedback and assistance throughout our writing process. Additional thanks to Sarah Brown Wessling, 2010 National Teacher of the Year, for writing the Foreword in which she introduces the book's content and clarifies its unique value.

Like the practice of teaching, constructing a book is a process of continuous refinement. The support of our colleagues and families has been instrumental in the completion of this project. For that we owe them our most sincere gratitude.

Trent. I have been blessed with the most amazing partners. Emily Grimm, my writing partner, has earned my deepest trust and respect in our three years of working and writing together. Teacher-driven observation exists because of her persistence in perfecting the core logic behind it—first for our partner schools, and now for this book. My business partner, Randy, has been more supportive of this book than I could have ever hoped. His peerless stamina and example of thinking big have kept our eyes on our ambitious writing goals. My life partner, Rosie, has not only read and critiqued every sentence in this book, but for years she has helped me hone the ideas in it through our nightly walks and noontime phone conversations. Her orientation for seeking feedback and self-improvement in her daily work are core principles on which teacher-driven observation was created. Words are insufficient for describing my love and admiration for her. And special thanks to my youngest partners—JT, Isaac, Kate, Henry, Philip, and Nora—for helping me keep it real. After writing all day, going home to wrestling matches and bike rides are just what the doctor ordered.

Emily. I have been truly fortunate to engage in this project with my colleague Trent Kaufman, who has the keen ability to defy math, such that his efforts and my own are greater than the sum of the individual parts. Both his passion for improving the culture of professional learning in education and his commitment to creating a resource that truly serves teachers have contributed to this project from inception to completion. My trail and life partner, David, has enriched my life in ways too innumerable to note here. His zest for adventure, patience, and sense of humor ground me (particularly on late nights of writing). I owe him my deepest thanks for his enduring companionship and support, both of which enabled this project and have carried me over many mountain peaks, both real and symbolic. I look forward to our next adventure—whatever it may be.

CONTENTS

FOREWORD

As the 2010 National Teacher of the Year, I have had the unique opportunity of talking with thousands of fellow educators about the state of American education. In these conversations, I noticed a trend that didn't honestly surprise me: many of them described feeling isolated in their classrooms and entrenched in their routines. However, when I asked these educators how they would shape the practice of education differently, I *was* surprised at how their insights began to dovetail. They expressed hope for a deliberate culture shift—for the ability to work in an environment of inquiry and collaboration within their schools.

I developed my wish list for American education from these conversations. I hope for schools where teachers are empowered to ask the toughest questions without fear of failing. I hope for schools where administrators get to immerse themselves in instruction as much as they must immerse themselves in the business of running a school. I hope for schools where colleagues consider each other trusted experts, willing to wear the same kind of transparent vulnerability with each other as they do with their students. I hope for schools where teachers have the kind of professional development that fuels their instruction because of the system, not in spite of it.

The kind of school I'm describing is not utopian. Across the country, there *are* schools that embody many elements of my wish list, to the benefit of students and educators alike. But there are far too many that don't.

The first step is to take a step—to find a way to help teachers see the power of learning not just from their own classrooms but also from the classrooms of others. In *The Transparent Teacher*, Trent Kaufman and Emily Dolci Grimm have given schools a blueprint for empowered professional development. When the nexus of growth becomes the teacher's own inquiry, Kaufman and Grimm aren't just suggesting that teachers take charge of a process; they're offering a way to create a learner-centered culture through the practice of teacher-driven observation. For teachers, this opportunity to cultivate learner dispositions is a chance to recast professional development (PD). No longer is PD something done *to* teachers; now it's done *by* them. With precise direction and clear purpose, the authors help teachers learn to zoom in and zoom out of their own classrooms, using classroom observation data to uncover the patterns left by teaching that advise deliberate instructional shifts. With thoughtful discussion on how to prepare for an observation, precise directions for implementing it, and insightful ways to sustain this work as it shifts school culture, this book will help you transform the way you think about your practice. In addition to the protocols and the specific advice for administrators, you'll be drawn in by Heather, Margaret, and Jay, whose story of teacher-driven observation makes this process come alive.

Teacher-driven observations help teachers become the empowered professionals they deserve to be. In moving professional development from the convention center to the classroom, Kaufman and Grimm are elevating us all to the status of learner.

Johnston, Iowa

February 2013

Sarah Brown Wessling
2010 National Teacher of the Year

THE TRANSPARENT TEACHER

INTRODUCTION

As we introduce *The Transparent Teacher* and teacher-driven observation to audiences of teachers and administrators, we find that they are interested in hearing the origins of this unique teacher-driven observation process. We'll share with you now the short narrative we offer them because it illustrates what is possible when a teacher takes charge of her learning and becomes transparent in her practice. Set during evaluation time when Trent was a brand-new high school assistant principal, this story provides the vision for what it means to take charge. In this story, you will find our motivations for writing this book and the power this process has to shift the culture of teaching. We predict that you'll see connections between the narrative and your own experiences as a teacher.

SHIFTING TEACHER OBSERVATIONS

I had been a high school assistant principal for all of three days when the principal gave me the list. I felt my heartbeat quicken as my eyes scanned the names of twenty-two teachers I was assigned to evaluate that year. My situation as an administrator holding this list was unique: several years back, I had been a new teacher at this same school, and a number of these teachers had mentored me. In my eyes, they were masters of the trade.

I was expected to make two visits to each classroom over the course of the school year. The first was an informal but scheduled observation, where I would observe the class at an appointed time and recommend areas for improvement. Later in the year I would drop in for the formal evaluation, during which I'd look for progress in the improvement area the teacher and I had chosen.

I'm not sure why the principal recommended I first observe Shelly, known as the best math teacher in the district. She was intimidating and really, really good. As the head of the union, she had both experience and influence. Maybe he thought that if I could survive this one, I'd be on my way. Maybe he told her to take it easy on me a little. Who knows? Frankly, I was less worried about the formal evaluation than about the first observation because the first required me to suggest areas for improvement without the structure of a rubric or set of criteria.

Most of my teachers, including Shelly, were teaching subjects I'd never taught, and many of them had far more classroom experience than I did. I lay awake in bed wondering how the observations might go and what it would take for me to add value to their teaching. Certainly I'd need to come up with something useful—if not brilliant—in order to prove myself as an effective administrator.

It came to me the next morning as I was driving to work. In graduate school, I'd taken a class that was directed toward administrators and described the importance of collecting objective data in the classroom. Instead of walking into these classrooms and observing whatever caught my attention, I would assign myself the role of data collector. I decided to take this idea one step further: because there are so many potential data sources in the classroom, I would focus specifically on collecting data that the teacher wanted. That approach felt exciting to me. It meant that I would need to communicate with each of these teachers before our observation and ask them what they were focusing on improving in their teaching.

When Shelly knocked on my office door the morning before our scheduled observation, I sat up straight. She sat down and crossed her legs carefully as I launched into an explanation of my plan to collect data during our observation in an area she was focused on improving. Her eyes brightened as she caught hold of the idea and told me, "In my classes recently, I've been focusing on how to improve my questioning. My goal is to engage more students in my basic math classes, and I believe that asking more application questions will help me accomplish that."

"I follow you completely," I responded. "Would it help you if I script all the application questions you ask during our observation?"

"I like that idea. Do you think you could also script what the students say in response? Then we could have a conversation afterward about what's actually going on in the classroom. We'll probably see some next steps I can take based on the data," she concluded, taking charge. "I'm up for that!"

I responded, making a mental note to brush up on Bloom's taxonomy before the observation, "See you in third period!" She nodded, smiled, and went off to class.

I arrived at her room with confidence born of clear purpose: I knew exactly what I was going to do during that observation, and I knew that it would add value. Over the next hour, I drained the ink from my pen, earnest in my commitment to support her by gathering data relevant to the area she had designated. As quickly as my ears picked up her questions and translated them to my fingers, she gathered responses from student after student.

Having filled my assignment with zest, I was equally confident when we debriefed the observation after school. Sitting in her classroom, we shared an extremely productive, data-based conversation. Because the data I had collected were at the heart of our conversation, she didn't feel threatened: we were reviewing teaching data, not evaluating the teacher. As we looked at the questions and student responses I'd scripted, we quickly noted the following:

- Around five students attempted to answer each application question. It took this many attempts at answering the questions for someone to respond appropriately.

- Of the ten application questions she asked in the one-hour period, fifteen of her twenty-eight students had attempted to answer one. This meant that many of the same students were attempting to answer the questions.

- The ten correct answers were given by four different students.

Shelly asked for my insight as an observer: "What were the other thirteen students doing during the lesson? Why were only four students able to answer my application questions?"

As we discussed the data, Shelly suggested a few things she could try. "Maybe if I chunk the questions into more digestible parts and begin to require everyone to answer them, I'll find the real value in these application questions." She fleshed out her plans and bounced ideas off me as she considered how the data I collected could help her improve. I was greatly relieved that I didn't have to be a math expert or even a teaching expert to be a productive observer.

Our interaction had a positive impact on my capacity as an observer. I began to take on the role of data collector, and the teachers I observed felt my commitment to helping them do better what they were already doing.

At Shelly's retirement party several years later, we talked about that observation experience. She laughed when I admitted how nervous I'd been and thanked me for making a difference in her professional development that year: "You know, when I learn a new strategy at a conference, there is a fifty-fifty chance it simply won't transfer to an effective practice in my classroom. Now I've found that when I have a colleague observe me implement a strategy in *my* classroom with *my* students, the likelihood that it sticks is almost 100 percent." As I nodded, she continued, "Working with you, I really felt that I took ownership of the observation process. You helped me improve an area I was already focused on, and the data you collected showed us the next steps."

As an educator, I took several important lessons from this experience with Shelly, and these lessons serve as the foundation for this book:

- The main ingredient for an effective observation experience is the disposition of the observed teacher. If the observed teacher wants to learn, the possibilities are unlimited.

- Being an effective observer is within everyone's reach. I didn't have to be brilliant or know something Shelly didn't. Most important, I didn't even have to be an administrator. I simply needed to be sincere in my desire to help, earnest in my data collection, and willing to engage in dialogue about the data.

- Shelly took charge and moved her professional development into her own classroom, in large part by becoming a transparent teacher with her classroom open to observation. She owned her professional development by declaring an area of focus and enlisting me to gather data. Clarifying these roles eliminated awkwardness from the postobservation debriefing: I had simply gathered data to help her answer her own questions about her teaching. Since I collected data rather than trying to opine about her teaching, we had a productive, nonthreatening conversation about teaching and learning in her classroom.

Since this time, I have founded Education Direction, an organization that teaches these and other data-driven education principles to hundreds of schools and districts.

THE TRANSPARENT TEACHER: TAKING CHARGE OF YOUR INSTRUCTION WITH PEER-COLLECTED CLASSROOM DATA

That title and subhead are a mouthful. To give you an idea of what we're really saying here, we'd like to explain the words we chose.

The teachers we work with often describe feeling frustrated with the professional development they receive. The strategies may be interesting, but they don't work consistently in the classroom. Professional development topics can be innovative and groundbreaking, but much gets lost in the space between the convention center (or where teachers received professional development training) and the classroom (where they put the strategies into practice).

This space is our niche—the gap we're bridging. We support teachers in taking charge. When teachers take charge of their professional development by moving it directly into their classrooms, they take charge of their own growth, effectiveness, and even overall job satisfaction. Using the techniques we present in this book for teacher-driven observation, teachers lead their professional learning inside their own classrooms.

Breaking down the professional isolation characteristic of the profession and opening up our classrooms—becoming transparent teachers—is a necessary part of moving professional development to our classrooms and into the context in which we work each day. As a teacher leading your own teacher-driven observation (TDO), you'll invite your peers to collaborate with you in observations in order to collect data. When you open your classroom to your peers, creating transparency around the teaching and learning that occurs there, you'll set the stage for your colleagues to collect classroom data. Having these data is like having eyes in the back of your head: they allow you to see into the blind spots of teaching that occur for every teacher. Instructing is a 100 percent mental capacity endeavor, so you miss details like how many times a student got out of his seat or what questions the students asked during the lesson. You answered those questions, but you don't know ultimately how many questions you posed, or whether the student questions reflected their collective understanding or confusion related to the topic.

Taking charge means that you decide what areas you'd like to focus on in your teaching. TDO gives you the tools to answer your questions as you collaborate with your colleagues. Taking charge means that you control who comes into your classroom and when. You guide the meetings and keep the data collected. We invite you to take charge of your teaching and situate your professional development in your classroom by reading this book.

HOW TO USE THIS BOOK

As you dive into the following chapters, you'll hear the voices and read about the experiences of hundreds of teachers engaged in TDO. We hope that the process offers you, as it has for them, a way of leading transformation in your teaching and improving student learning.

The Transparent Teacher will be a rich resource for you in implementing TDO. So that you get the most out of it, the remainder of this Introduction describes the three parts of the book, gives you an idea of where to start reading, and details key chapter features. It also highlights the chapter summaries and study questions at the end of the book that may prove relevant for your personal review or for a book study group.

Parts 1 Through 3

Part 1, "Preparing," explores the purpose of TDO and topics relevant to planning for its implementation in chapters 1 and 2. Together these chapters provide a context for what TDO can do for your teaching and the professional culture in your school. They also address the preparation that best sets you up for success. Through the exploration of these topics, you'll meet Heather, a seventh-grade math teacher who is looking for a meaningful way to apply her professional learning to the unique context of her classroom. By the end of part 1, you will be ready to dig into the specific steps of TDO.

Chapters 3 through 5 in part 2, "Implementing," detail each of the three steps of TDO. Each chapter explains how to engage in one step of the process, providing examples and tips that support implementation. You'll continue to follow Heather's journey as she engages in the TDO process. Her experiences provide a comprehensive, insider view of the process from start to finish. You'll also read about how other teachers have applied the core principles of TDO in their work. By the time you finish part 2, you'll have a clear vision of how TDO can support your learning and the instruction in your classroom. You may even feel prepared to begin a round of TDO.

Chapters 6 through 8 in part 3, "Sustaining," aim to answer your questions, from, "How do I find the time to implement this process?" to, "How might this process look across my grade-level team?" Principals who are interested in kicking off TDO schoolwide will find particular value in chapter 7, the only chapter written directly to administrators. The final chapter provides a narrative of a large, comprehensive high school that implemented TDO across a faculty of 170 teachers. This case study illustrates the challenges and successes that can occur when teachers engage in TDO.

Finally, the epilogue examines how the practice of TDO relates to the work of professional learning communities (PLCs), an increasingly common collaborative structure in schools. If PLCs exist among your faculty, the epilogue will provide value in examining how TDO can support your existing work. Even if a PLC structure is not in place, this chapter will help you see how TDO can propel collaborative work in your school.

Where to Start Reading

Your role in your school and your existing comfort with having observers collaborate with you about your teaching will inform how you use this book. Teachers and administrators who are brand new to the concept of TDO will find it most helpful to begin with parts 1 and 2, moving on to part 3 when they are ready for implementation. If you're intrigued by the concept and ready to learn more about the practices themselves, you may find it most helpful to begin with part 2 in order to build your understanding of the process itself.

Chapter Features

Each chapter contains text boxes that highlight key points. These points are the big things to remember about TDO and are useful for in-text navigation and review.

Each chapter also contains at least two boxes titled "A Note to Principals" that highlight information that is relevant from the point of view of principals. Principals who are reading this book might flip through the chapters to read those boxes first and then look for more detail as is relevant. Because chapter 7 is dedicated to addressing principals, there are no principal boxes in that chapter.

A "Common Missteps" section follows the main body of each chapter in most of the chapters in parts 2 and 3. We've culled these from the experiences of hundreds of teachers across dozens of schools. You'll find it helpful to take note of these not only during your initial reading but also to revisit these as you engage in the practice—both in its infancy and development.

Chapter Summaries and Study Questions

If you've read this book before or just prefer to begin with more of a quick point version, flip to the back of the book and read the chapter summaries provided there. These summaries may give you an idea of which chapter you'd like to refer to for greater detail. We've also provided study questions that connect directly with each chapter. These questions are designed to encourage deeper thinking about the concepts in the chapters and promote personal application. Any teacher working with TDO can benefit from thinking through these questions. They can also be used in more formal book study gatherings or graduate school courses.

FINAL THOUGHTS

We are confident that you'll find in the pages ahead both the vision and the resources for creating a professional, job-embedded learning experience inside your own classroom that empowers you to take charge of your teaching and equips you to become a transparent teacher.

PART ONE

Preparing

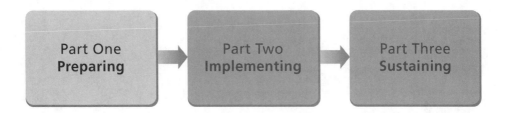

CHAPTER ONE

TEACHER-DRIVEN OBSERVATION FOR PROFESSIONAL LEARNING

Heather reflects on her first four years of teaching as she drives to school on a fall morning. She enjoys her talkative, sometimes gawky, often charming students—they are the reason she entered the profession as a bright-eyed college graduate. Heather appreciates the challenges of her profession—particularly as she teaches mathematics to so many students with unique needs—and she often wonders about the next stage in her development as a teacher. Great teachers really inspire her, and she's cultivating the qualities they express, but her classroom often seems like an isolated place. As weeks turn into months, she is never exactly certain that she's making a difference. Sure, she's teaching through the lesson manuals and tracking her students' progress, but she wishes there were a way to get feedback on how she is progressing as a teacher. Administrators have made their way into her classroom over the years for formal, evaluative observations, and she's always gotten high marks, but those observations haven't had a meaningful impact on her teaching.

Her school provides professional development on various topics, such as literacy strategies, or the district's newest online grading software. Heather regularly attends these sessions, but she feels unsure of her progress even when she implements the new strategies as well as she can in her classroom. No one is there to observe her or reinforce her efforts if she's doing well, and generally the school doesn't provide any follow-up to support ongoing implementation. Certainly her students don't bother to say, "Wow, I really appreciated how you used the gradual release of responsibility technique in our class this morning!" She smiles at the thought.

It's surprising, she reflects, that a profession centered on student learning doesn't focus as much on fostering learning opportunities for its teachers. Like some of the veteran teachers in the building, Heather feels increasingly frustrated with the professional development process because the trainings are so detached from her daily work with students. Although the topics often interest Heather, she doesn't know how to embed new strategies in her instruction and classroom routines.

As she pulls into the school parking lot, Heather commits to figuring it out this school year: she realizes she needs to take charge of her professional learning in a way that will stimulate her professional growth and satisfaction for years to come.

LEARNING IN THE CLASSROOM

Teaching is a profession that lives inside you, driving you to do better every day. We know this firsthand from the years we spent in the classroom. Like you, we regularly invested time outside class thinking about how we could engage a particular student who seemed to be perpetually off task. Before our students arrived in the morning, we found ourselves wondering how to make a particular concept more accessible to the students that day. Our students meant everything to us. They drove us crazy, ran us ragged, taxed our minds, and completely filled our hearts. Regardless of whether this is your first year teaching or your twentieth, these experiences may resonate with you to some degree. Nearly every teacher we've met shares one thing in common: a desire to improve—to become better equipped to make a meaningful difference with his or her students.

Because of this common improvement disposition among teachers, chances are good that you are already engaged in many simultaneous efforts to improve. Perhaps you have recently attended a conference or workshop. You may share strategies or assessments with your colleagues over lunch. Likely you tailor lesson plans from one year to the next to meet students' unique learning needs. In these and so many other ways, you continuously take on the challenge of improving your craft. However, like Heather, you are essentially on your own as you enter your classroom each day. Most teachers find themselves without the tools for measuring whether they are improving. They lack a method for examining their instruction as it happens—in their classrooms, with their students, and as they deliver their content.

This book proposes a step-by-step method to fill that gap because what you do each day in the classroom matters. In fact, research decisively concludes that no school element is more critical to student achievement than you, the teacher, are.[1] And yet opportunities for meaningful professional development—for improving what you do in the classroom each day—so often fall short.

THE STATE OF PROFESSIONAL DEVELOPMENT

As the first term progresses, Heather identifies a problematic pattern in her math classes: students are correctly solving problems as they work in small groups of two to three but consistently struggling on unit assessments. She wonders if she's failing to give them adequate independent practice prior to the assessment. Recently she attended a workshop on using gradual release of responsibility as a tool for building student proficiency. This strategy includes teacher modeling ("I do"), shared engagement in the task ("we do"), and students' independent practice ("you do").

Heather has been implementing elements of the strategy for years, but now she's decided to focus on the component of releasing responsibility to her students in order to bolster their performance. As she implements this strategy in her classroom, she wonders if she's using it effectively. It's surprising how much more complex the process feels in the context of her classroom, content, and students than it felt in the workshop setting. *This would be a good time for me to have eyes in the back of my head*, she thinks, *so I could really see how the release is working for my students*.

In theory, professional development (PD) is a great idea. In workshops, seminars, and meetings, PD infuses the teaching world with ideas and tools designed to make a difference. Unfortunately, that concept goes only so far. In practice, traditional approaches to PD fall short of having a deep impact on what teachers do in the classroom. And you can be sure that if PD fails to reach teachers, it also fails to reach students.

Key Point

If professional development fails to reach teachers, you can be sure it also fails to reach students.

In order to understand this problem, let's look at three reasons that PD generally isn't working as it occurs: teachers play the role of passive recipient, find that transferring strategies from training to the classroom presents a challenge, and lack opportunities to practice and refine new strategies. As you read the following sections, consider your own experiences with PD and see where this information hits home for you.

Teachers' Roles as Passive Recipients

During our years as teachers, we observed a trend at the beginning of each school year. As we set up our classrooms and waited in line for the photocopiers, we wondered what our schools would choose to focus on this year. Inevitably, on the opening day of school, our superintendent or principal would share the book he had read or the conference he had attended that sparked the year's improvement initiative. Ideas ranged from a new collaborative structure to a set of literacy strategies and always came soaked in the leader's enthusiasm. However, enthusiasm among teachers for the idea of the year was notably minimal: we were wondering how this initiative would equip us to more effectively face the challenges we experienced with our students and our content.

The shortcomings of this approach to PD are clear: PD opportunities that fail to solicit your input and experiences in the classroom place you in the role of passive recipient. Research notes that this is one of the "chief limitations of conventional models of professional development."[2] It's not surprising. When your voice and perspective are not guiding the focus of professional development, those efforts aren't likely to genuinely reflect the challenges you experience in your classroom. It is no wonder that when teachers sit as the idle recipients of content handed to them that does not reflect their own challenges and interests, this content will fail to permeate classroom walls and create meaningful improvements in teaching and learning.

Teachers' roles as passive recipients of professional development contribute to a lack of sustainability for these efforts. Most veteran teachers know they will remain at their school longer than the current leaders will. A revolving door of initiatives occurs when the focus of professional development shifts with each leader. This regular shift in focus, which characterizes the profession, prevents teachers from having the time to transform teaching and learning with each initiative.

Furthermore, when teachers are on the sidelines of PD decisions, they are unlikely to buy into the decisions that others make (particularly if the decision makers do not share their day-to-day classroom experiences).

A NOTE TO PRINCIPALS

You hold many, if not all, of the keys to professional development practices in your school. As you read this section and the next, consider how you can improve your current PD practices. For example, reflect on how you might use teacher-driven observation to enhance those practices by making it a response to teachers' identified needs, applicable in the classroom, and sustained over a broad time frame such that teachers have time to practice and refine new strategies.

Teachers and principals alike cite a lack of buy-in as an impediment to change. When leaders fail to solicit teachers' realities in the classroom and professional perspective as a starting point for PD efforts, teachers are not likely to engage meaningfully in these opportunities.

Education leader Tony Wagner aptly emphasizes that not only buy-in but ownership is critical to the success of school improvement efforts. He notes that "just as good teachers create classrooms in which students construct new knowledge, leaders must provide learning opportunities that enable teachers to 'construct' a new understanding of the world, their students, and their craft—and so enable them to 'own' both the problem and the solution rather than being coerced into 'buying' someone else's."[3]

When leaders create space for teachers to inform the focus of PD efforts, teachers will have ownership of these topics. It's not surprising, then, when these topics translate into instructional improvements.

As long as teachers remain passive recipients of PD, it will fall short of its intended impact. When leaders give teachers the reins to direct their learning, PD gains sufficient traction to improve instruction and impact student learning.

Transfer from Training to the Classroom

Learning a skill in one setting does not ensure application in another. To illustrate this point, imagine asking a beginning algebra student who has mastered a textbook problem to use a mathematical equation to describe a real-life decision. With math and with instruction, it's challenging to transfer learning from one context to another. This reality is problematic for current PD efforts. Teachers work hard to transfer learning from the training session to the classroom but regularly find themselves up against a big challenge in the process.

Transfer is particularly difficult when the PD itself is theoretical in nature, that is, offering ideas over strategies. Research notes that PD topics "are often conceptually and practically far removed from their classrooms."[4] Even when professional developers offer classroom-based and practical approaches to learning using classroom examples through role play, video, and examples, it is easy for learning to get lost between the conference center and the classroom. Just as with a math problem, your understanding may suddenly become hazier when you are implementing a strategy in a new context.

Each classroom is a new context. The dynamic nature of individual students and the unique culture that develops in a classroom require teachers to thoughtfully apply various strategies in each class every day. Any teacher who has used an identical lesson plan and strategies during different periods of the same school day can attest that effectiveness is connected with the powerful variables of student personalities, learning styles, and time of the day. The postlunch "food coma," a characteristically quiet group of students, or the energy that emerges after gym class will require variations in instructional strategies.

"Teaching occurs in particulars—particular students interacting with particular teachers over particular ideas in particular circumstances."[5] These classroom particulars present a challenge for traditional approaches to PD, because the one-size-fits-all approach cannot address the specifics of each classroom. Certainly talking about the implementation of a strategy among colleagues in a conference room presents less complexity than implementing that same strategy in a classroom of twenty-five sixth graders. And it is often not until we are back in our classrooms, surrounded by those twenty-five students, that we see the complexities of implementation. There is simply no way to replicate that experience in a PD setting.

Key Point

When professional development interfaces with classroom instruction, it can tailor to particulars—helping teachers bridge the gap between theory and practice.

Professional development removed from the classroom is analogous to teaching someone to swim using only a Power-Point presentation. An aspiring swimmer needs both context-specific instruction and practice. Similarly, PD isolated to a conference room cannot deeply explore classroom application of new tools or strategies as they relate to your own students, content, and classroom. The most effective way to reduce the transfer required of most PD is to move it into the space where teaching occurs: the classroom. You spend most of your time in the classroom, so it makes sense that the most powerful professional learning happens right there, rather than in the cafeteria or a convention center. Classroom-based PD also facilitates observation of teaching, which can occur only when we open our doors and make our instruction transparent to colleagues.[6] When PD interfaces with your classroom instruction, it can tailor to particulars—helping you bridge the gap between theory and practice. This is the kind of PD we describe in the following chapters for you to use in your classroom.

A Lack of Opportunities to Practice and Refine New Strategies

Would you expect your students to master new content after only one lesson or without multiple rounds of attempts (from them) and feedback (from you)? As a teacher, you know that applied and deliberate practice is a critical component of effective teaching and learning. If your experiences are anything like our own, you've sat through countless one-shot PD sessions covering content from the latest computer software, to student engagement strategies, to a new behavioral referral system, and many other topics in between. Whether the content was immediately relevant to your classroom, the capacity for an isolated workshop to have a deep impact on classroom instruction is low. "One-shot workshops and prepackaged seminars, although potentially effective for creating awareness and building discrete skills, are insufficient for facilitating teacher collaboration and change."[7] And yet it is a rare teacher who participates in PD that explores consistent material over a period of time and includes rounds of practice and feedback.

Expecting a teacher to implement new strategies without practicing specific application is akin to expecting an artist to paint like Van Gogh or Picasso without practicing with a brush, or expecting an athlete to play like a professional after watching a game tape but not actually playing on a field. Athletes develop their skill by studying the work of others and by practicing—over, and over, and over—and by using observers' feedback to refine their technique. It only makes sense that teaching should require the same practice, feedback, reflection, and precision. This approach demands PD that includes opportunities for ongoing classroom application and refinement.

All too frequently, after PD, teachers go back to their rooms left to tackle implementation in isolation. This approach is problematic because it provides "almost no opportunity for teachers to engage in continuous and sustained learning about their practice in the setting in which they actually work, observing and being observed by their colleagues in their own classrooms and in the classrooms of other teachers in other schools confronting similar problems of practice."[8] Without collaboration, implementation stagnates, and without feedback, teachers are unable to refine their implementation to best suit student learning.

Deliberate practice—practice during which "performance is carefully monitored to provide cues for ways to improve it further"—is a metacognitive endeavor.[9] Any teacher can attest to the challenge of monitoring his or her own instruction in real time, in addition to addressing the learning needs of twenty-five students. Thus, deliberate practice is most effective when it is approached collaboratively, with the perspective and expertise of others. Athletes receive feedback from coaches, and surgeons accept review from peers, but teaching has historically been an isolated profession. Teachers can be more effective when they receive meaningful feedback about their work from sustained, collaborative, and job-embedded opportunities for learning. Unfortunately, traditional approaches to PD have fallen short of this vision.

Without formal opportunities for practice and refinement, your ability to apply your learning can be overshadowed by the daily demands of your classroom. In a class period where three students are patiently (or sometimes not so patiently) waiting to ask questions simultaneously, a fire drill interrupts the pace of your lesson, and two students have already completed the day's assignment, implementing and reflecting on a new strategy falls low on your to-do list. When PD includes time for deliberate practice in collaboration with your colleagues, it provides the time to invest in doing what you do better. That, after all, is the purpose of PD.

TEACHER-DRIVEN OBSERVATION

After grading another set of tests with disappointing results, Heather heads out to the teacher's lounge to pick up a soda. *What do you do when it's just not working?* she asks herself. *There's got to be something I'm missing.* In the lounge, she shares her frustrations with two colleagues: Jay, a seventh-grade social studies teacher, and Margaret, a second-year math teacher who has become a close friend: "At the end of this unit, I was confident my students had developed the skills necessary to calculate surface area, but clearly I missed the mark. They did it well in groups, but they are still struggling when it comes time for them to demonstrate mastery on their own. I've got to change what I am doing. I've started being more intentional about the gradual release method we reviewed on our last day of PD, but I wish I could learn to implement it more effectively." Jay and Margaret nod, empathizing with the challenge Heather is facing.

As they discuss potential strategies she could try, Heather has an idea. Maybe Jay and Margaret can watch her teach for a short period of time and offer their insights. They'd be able to see what was happening in the classroom and might find clues to what she could do better. *It could be awkward to have them come in my room*, Heather thinks. But then she remembers hearing Fernando, a colleague in a neighboring district, talk about how his school does this sort of thing all the time. He'd mentioned a process called teacher-driven observation, but she'd have to ask him about the specifics. If it worked in his school, maybe it could work in her classroom. Drawing a deep breath, she poses the question: "Jay, Margaret, would you be willing to come into my classroom and observe my instruction with my students? I think you'd be able to gather what's going on, and maybe together we could come up with ways I can more effectively release responsibility." They agree.

The shortcomings of traditional approaches to PD call for change. However, they also highlight the opportunities that can exist when PD moves into the classroom and teachers direct their own learning. Teacher-driven observation (TDO) creates this opportunity. As you identify a focus area and plan an observation in your classroom, TDO gives you the reins to direct your learning, allows you to practice and refine your instructional approaches, and plants PD firmly in the classroom.

You've been through observations before; they are a fixture of most teachers' professional tenure. We invite you to put those experiences (whether positive or negative) on the shelf and open your mind to a new experience. Becoming a transparent teacher through teacher-driven observation is different in two ways from every other observation you've done. First, as the lead teacher, you take charge by moving your PD into your classroom. Second, whereas the observations you've experienced in the past have probably been for evaluation purposes or identifying best practices, teacher-driven observation is all about collecting and examining classroom data to inform and improve your own instruction.

Key Point

In TDO, the primary learning value is for the observed teacher.

Your role as a lead teacher or an observer in TDO differs distinctly from the roles you have played in other observation models. These differences show up in three areas: the purpose of the observation, who directs the process, and who gains value as the primary learner. Figure 1.1 highlights these elements.

The differences noted between teacher-driven observation and other observation models are critical, and we explore them in more detail in the next chapter.

		Purpose	Who Directs the Process	Recipient of the Primary Learning Value
	Common observation models	Observe model classroom	Observer	Observer
		Evaluate teacher effectiveness	Administrator	Administrator
TDO	**Teacher-driven observation**	Collect data to inform and improve individual instruction	Observed teacher	Observed teacher

FIGURE 1.1. Teacher-Driven Observation Versus Common Observation Models

Before we get there, however, let's examine how the TDO process addresses the shortfalls of traditional approaches to PD. Each of these factors will equip you to prepare for TDO with clarity about how it can contribute to your professional learning and growth:

- *TDO gives teachers a process for leading their learning.* It places you firmly in charge of your professional learning. TDO speaks directly to the challenges you face in your classroom because you identify the focus for your observation, and you direct the attention of your observers to that focus. Through this process, PD responds to the needs you experience in your classroom, with your students, in your content area. Being in charge of your learning doesn't mean that you ignore the innovative ideas you may learn at PD sessions you attend outside your classroom. Instead, TDO gives you a chance to focus on the new ideas that will make the biggest difference for your students.

- *TDO puts professional learning in the classroom context.* It eliminates the challenge of transfer as you engage in PD in the context of your own classroom. The data your observers collect provide a foundation for learning that is immediately relevant: the data illustrate the relationship between your teaching and your students' learning, given your content area and grade level. These data enable professional learning that informs your ability to make changes in your classroom right away.

- *TDO creates collaborative opportunities to practice and refine strategies.* It recognizes that learning a strategy requires more than reading or hearing about it. TDO goes one step further by providing a context for applying your learning and refining it over time. When teachers enter one another's classrooms focused on collecting and examining data together, they empower each other to reflect and refine instruction. Through focused opportunities for deliberate practice, TDO encourages the self-reflection that is critical to mastering any complex practice.

TAKING CHARGE

Although Heather is nervous about her colleagues' visit to her classroom, she feels confident that the data they'll gather will provide her with a valuable perspective on her focus area. When she's in the midst of teaching, her mind is attentive to how she's delivering the lesson to her students. Being present in teaching, however, means that she can't at the same time explore the dynamics between her instruction and student learning. She can't tell, for instance, how well she's releasing responsibility to her students so that they can perform the calculations on their own. That's where she knows her colleagues' eyes and ears can make the difference.

Key Point

In teacher-driven observation, the lead teacher identifies the focus of the observation.

Despite some uncertainly, Heather can see how opening her door and engaging in a conversation about her classroom with her colleagues can provide the information she's been missing. *This is the sort of professional support I need*, she realizes. *After all those training sessions, having my colleagues come into my classroom and watch my implementation will not only help me gauge my progress, but will encourage me to sustain the process over time*.

As teachers, you can probably identify with Heather's experience even if you haven't tried TDO. It can be nerve-wracking to have colleagues, administrators, or anyone else enter your classroom. But there undoubtedly have been moments as you are teaching when you wish you had an extra set of eyes and ears to see what's really going on for the students. How well are they getting what you're up there teaching? You're in high-output mode to deliver an interesting, content-based lesson, and in that mode, it's hard to take stock of all the complex elements of teaching and student learning.

Having extra eyes and ears can make all the difference in your classroom. Heather knows that her peer observers will pick up on what she can't see because her mind and senses are occupied with teaching. As they write down the questions she and her students ask, focusing on the dynamics of the interaction, this scripting will hold clues to ways she can improve her teaching and her students' learning. TDO becomes her tool for bridging the gap—seeing into the otherwise inaccessible space of what's really going on while she is teaching.

Once you get a taste of the information available using TDO, you may find it hard to live without it. We've seen that as teachers implement TDO, it becomes an essential practice for them. We've also noticed that as other teachers in the school get wind of what's going on in TDO teams, they want in on the action, and TDO begins to permeate all classrooms. From there, things take off. A high school chemistry teacher and English teacher collaborate to improve student engagement techniques. Third-, fourth-, and fifth-grade teachers observe one another to refine alignment across grade levels. Their collaboration dissolves the walls that commonly exist between different content areas and grade levels and magnifies opportunities for growth. Teachers engage with colleagues in professional collaborative practice by innovatively structuring observations and conversations.

We've written this book in support of this ambitious—and possible—vision. At this point, we offer a few tips for you as you take charge of implementing your own TDO: begin with the end in mind, expect cultural change because it comes with the territory, and recognize the potential that TDO has to interface with professional learning communities. Everyone's experience implementing TDO will be different, but as you read these tips, you'll see what can apply to your situation.

Begin with the End in Mind

What's the end goal of TDO? By moving PD from the convention center to the classroom, TDO addresses many common shortcomings of traditional PD. However, the objective is not simply to improve PD; it's to enable you to take charge of your professional learning experience. This process will enable you to collect and analyze data that can inform your teaching and improve your students' learning.

That is no small goal. Riveting your focus on this goal will guide you through all the logistics and potential emotional hurdles you may encounter. As you read the following chapters, you'll find support for every step of the way.

Expect Cultural Change

Anytime you make a change, it stimulates changes around you. It's like tossing a pebble (TDO) into a pond (your school) and watching ripples expand in widening rings. The TDO process challenges the one-shot construction of PD, thereby opening a space for relevant, classroom-based, job-embedded professional learning. It also unmasks the profession of teaching itself—where we practice a "process of private trial and error" over a "publicly deliberative process of inquiry and experiment."[10] The

Key Point

The point of teacher-driven observation is to enable you to take charge of your professional learning by collecting and analyzing data that can inform your teaching and improve your students' learning.

practices we outline throughout this book are designed to turn the old culture of private classrooms into a new culture of transparent practice—one in which teachers can build professional relationships and learn from one another, honing their craft and implementing best techniques.

TDO also revises teachers' expectations for classroom observations. Instead of seeing observation as a tool for evaluation—more of a "gotcha" than an opportunity for real growth—TDO enables teachers to use observation as a tool for their own learning. We are the first to admit that we propose ambitious work. However, we highlight dozens of examples in this book illustrating how this work can create true change in the culture of your school.

Recognize the Potential to Interface with Professional Learning Communities

If your school has implemented professional learning communities (PLCs), you might be wondering how TDO works with them. In fact, you don't need to have PLCs at your school in order to implement TDO; however, they can work well together.

PLCs have increasingly gained traction as a structure and practice for supporting improvements in teaching and learning. While the implementation of the model varies, PLCs are commonplace in many districts, which makes their mention important within the context of TDO. Their guiding objectives—collaborative inquiry into and a focus on improving learning for all students grounded in a clear and collective vision—are directly aligned with the content we explore throughout the remaining chapters.

A NOTE TO PRINCIPALS

The premise of PLCs dovetails precisely with the objective of TDO: it asserts that "if the organization is to become more effective in helping all students learn, the adults in the organization must also be continually learning."[11] These shared goals make the framework for PLCs and TDO particularly compatible. We suggest that TDO can become a critical piece of the work of PLCs, particularly as these communities use evidence of student performance to inform practice. The Epilogue discusses potential interactions between PLCs and TDO.

It's important to note that PLCs are not a prerequisite for implementing a productive TDO process. We have seen teachers in schools with formal existing

---

Key Point

The TDO process and PLCs can work well together, but you don't have to have PLCs in order to implement TDO at your school. See the Epilogue for more ideas on integrating PLCs with TDO.

---

structures for teacher collaboration, like those within the design of PLCs, implement TDO. We have also seen schools succeed with TDO without an existing structure for common planning time. So while the TDO process nests well into the framework of PLCs or other common planning time frameworks, rounds of TDO can also stand alone.

FINAL THOUGHTS

In the long run, TDO can change the culture of your school in large and important ways. Let that vision excite and motivate you, but don't get overwhelmed. By reading this book, you're making the first steps of your journey. You already have the framework you need right in your classroom and with your colleagues. They'll collaborate with you along the way. Initiating the work does not require creating a perfect model, but each step moves you toward a meaningful practice for your professional learning.

In the following chapters, we provide a context for beginning and the tools for your journey. Through the experiences of classroom teachers, we illustrate the power of taking charge of your professional learning by opening your practice to your peers and becoming a transparent teacher.

Key Point

Just do it! Initiating TDO does not require creating a perfect model, but each step moves you toward a meaningful practice for your professional learning.

CHAPTER TWO
PREPARING FOR TEACHER-DRIVEN OBSERVATION

Heather knows she's taken a big step as soon as the words leave her mouth. By inviting Jay and Margaret into her classroom to observe her teaching, she knows she'll get fresh insight through the data they collect. That's what matters: having those data and collaborating with her colleagues will help her see what's happening in her classroom. Maybe they'll help her come up with next steps that make the difference in her students' learning. That's her goal.

She has a few butterflies in her stomach, but there's no turning back. Looking forward, Heather decides to make sure she's clear on her purpose: if she has a purpose in place, Jay and Margaret will be well situated to help her. After school that day, she calls Fernando to learn more about teacher-driven observation (TDO). He's excited to talk. He tells her that it's different from any other observation process he's participated in. "You know how administrators come in, check a few boxes on their papers, and leave?" he asks. "Well, this is totally different. Instead of the observer evaluating you, you're in charge. You get to define your focus area for the observation, choose who you want to observe you, and what data collection method they'll use. It's all about your taking charge and getting the data you need to learn what you want to know about your classroom." Heather lets this sink in. It sounds entirely different from the professional development sessions she's used to attending, where she and her colleagues sit in the cafeteria and listen to presentations on new strategies. This is professional development in real time in the center ring.

Imagine two hikers preparing to head out for a week on the Appalachian Trail. Two million to 3 million people walk a portion of the trail every year. Measuring roughly 2,180 miles in length, it is one of the world's longest continuously marked footpaths. Hikers' goals vary greatly. Some people walk the entire trail in a continuous journey, while others cover just a section of it. What supplies should they put in their backpacks? What shoes should they wear? What portion of the trail will they cover? All of these important details vary according to their goals.

Any new pursuit—whether hiking the Appalachian Trail or engaging in TDO (and, trust us, TDO is much less painful)—benefits from having a clearly defined purpose. The specific purpose set forth for an activity has an impact on all subsequent steps of the process. Imagine now that two hikers have different goals in mind: both are preparing to hike some portion of the trail but one is looking for a physical challenge of high-mileage days and the other wants to enjoy a scenic walk. The hikers' subsequent planning—from what gear they pack, to where they enter and exit the trail, to their physical conditioning—will reflect their chosen purpose.

> **Key Point**
>
> *A fundamental tenet of teacher-driven observation is to collect and examine data that inform and improve both teaching and learning.*

If in some twist of fate they switched backpacks at the airport, the serious hiker would be as dismayed to find a heavy camera and leather-bound journal as the scenic hiker would be to discover the minimalist tarp and lightweight freeze-dried food. Likewise, if neither had clarified her purpose and packed accordingly, both would be ill prepared for their journey. As with hiking, so with the TDO process: tailoring your preparation to your stated goals makes it much easier to meet the objectives of the journey.

As a teacher preparing to participate in TDO observation, you'll want to get clear on what its purpose is and what it is not. You'll benefit from being familiar with the process—just as hiking a trail is easier when you know what's around the bend. You'll want to be familiar with the roles of lead teacher and observer so you'll know what to expect when it's your turn. Clarifying the purpose, process, and roles of TDO will prepare you to become a transparent teacher—to engage in the practice and facilitate the learning you seek.

THE PURPOSE OF TEACHER-DRIVEN OBSERVATION

Observation is a part of most teachers' professional tenure at one point or another. These experiences can cloud our understanding of the purpose of TDO. In fact, TDO serves a purpose that is different from these other observation experiences.

It is a nonevaluative process whose purpose is to collect and examine classroom data to inform and improve instruction. That's the short answer. The longer answer takes shape in the following sections.

An Opening of Classroom Doors from the Inside, Not the Outside

Unlike many other observation models where the observers lead the learning, TDO situates the observed teacher as the leader of the observation. She identifies the focus of the observation, the methods for data collection, and the context for the observation. As a transparent teacher, she opens her classroom door and invites her colleagues in. This differs from best-practice observation models where observers decide whom they will observe and what they're looking for as they build their instructional tools and strategies.

A NOTE TO PRINCIPALS

As you introduce TDO to your faculty, we recommend you start by discussing each component of this section on the purpose of TDO. Beginning in this way will kick off your school's introduction to TDO with the right tone.

This fundamental shift in the role of the observed and lead teacher is a critical element of TDO. It places the observed teacher as the leader of the observation, empowering her to navigate her learning. Thinking through this shift in the context of your teaching, imagine how your relationship with your observers changes when you are in the driver's seat. It is an entirely different experience than the typical evaluation. In our experience, the productivity of this observer–observed teacher relationship is greatly magnified when your observers become your team members—as they become gatherers of the data that build your success.

About Gathering Data for Improvement, Not for Accountability.

Teachers' experiences with observation are most frequently linked to evaluation. In fact, for many teachers, their only experience opening their classroom doors to observers is for evaluative purposes. That's why it's easy to be confused initially about the purpose of TDO. Richardson states: "The perceived association between peer observations and evaluations is deeply entrenched in the entire educational community."[1] Unfortunately, when participants mistakenly treat TDO as an accountability procedure rather than an improvement process, they undermine its purpose. One reason is that teachers may be tentative or downright resistant to engage in a process they view as evaluative. In other words, fear of evaluation, not of the observation itself, may steer teachers away from exploring the process.

A second reason is that teachers who enter the TDO process with an evaluative purpose in mind can undermine it: lead teachers will fail to take the reins instead deferring to observers, and observers will make judgments rather than collect data from their classroom visit.

Instead of using observation as a means for measurement, TDO rescripts observation as a tool you can use to see into your classroom and into your students' learning from a vantage point other than your spot at the front of the room. Teaching is a 100 percent mental capacity job, so the observers become eyes and ears for gathering information that you want to collect but simply cannot focus on while you're teaching. With this information, you can improve your teaching and your students' learning.

Grounded in Formative, Not Summative, Data

Summative data draw conclusions; formative data offer real-time insight. Teacher-driven observation is not the place to draw conclusions about the quality of a teacher's instruction. Instead of fostering conversations that deal in final analysis, such as, "Was his teaching effective?" TDO creates an opportunity to dig into the data at hand and explore the relationship between teaching and student learning. In other words, having your instruction deemed effective might feel good, but it does little to help you know what specific practices you could replicate, refine, or adopt. Classroom observation data are similar to student assessment data in their utility for teachers. Summative, end-of-year student performance data may be helpful to capture trends, but they do little to inform teachers on how to improve their instruction in the classroom immediately. But reviewing student classwork can provide insights that contribute to immediate instructional responses. Teacher-driven observation focuses on the collection of actionable, real-time, formative classroom data, equipping teachers to make meaningful improvements to their instruction tomorrow.

A Way to Do Better What You're Already Doing, Not an Add-On or Stand-Alone Practice

Often schools implement new programs and initiatives without fully considering how they support each other. This can be overwhelming for teachers, who end up with numerous items to manage in addition to teaching. Fortunately, TDO can help you unify the items you're already working with. Let's say your school is implementing Common Core State Standards. TDO provides a process for you to examine how you're implementing these standards into your practice. Can TDO contribute to classroom implementation if your department is focusing on improving instructional strategies for English language learners? What if the department is focusing on developing students' higher-order thinking skills? Can TDO make a difference there? Definitely. By collecting data and examining what happens in the classroom, TDO helps teachers do better what is already required of them. It is not an add-on but rather a practice for teacher-directed professional learning to embed in existing work. Table 2.1 illustrates some of the many ways TDO can enhance your instructional efforts.

It's easy to see how teachers might initially be unclear about the value of TDO. *Who needs more work or extra evaluative observations?* they might ask. If that's their perception of TDO, they won't be able to reap the rewards of this valuable process. Sometimes a teacher's preconceived ideas of classroom observation can

TABLE 2.1 WAYS IN WHICH TDO CAN ENHANCE YOUR EXISTING WORK

If Your School Is . . .	You Can Use TDO to . . .
Already implementing strategies to address the needs of English language learners	Examine the relationship between these strategies and student learning for English language learners in order to refine and improve implementation
Focused on increasing students' higher-order thinking skills	Examine the rigor of learning opportunities in your classroom and explore the application of strategies that effectively support your students' development of higher-order thinking skills
Invested in the classroom implementation of the Common Core State Standards	Identify a standard that presents challenge or complexity and use TDO to explore your instruction and its relationship to student learning within this standard
Working in professional learning communities to examine student work to identify instructional interventions	Take your professional learning communities a level deeper by collaboratively examining and refining the implementation of identified interventions in the classroom
Introducing a new teacher evaluation model	Identify an area of the new framework in which you would like to improve and use TDO as a process for refining practice in this area
Differentiating instruction as part of response to intervention	Use TDO to examine the relationship between instruction and student learning for students identified for interventions

keep him from getting full value from the TDO process. Here's where you can make the difference: you'll be able to leverage TDO for your own improvement when you view it as a process for teacher-directed professional learning. As you read through this and the following chapters, you'll be able to differentiate the purpose of TDO and thereby shape your colleagues' perceptions of it.

COMMUNICATING THE PURPOSE OF TDO

Consider for a moment that you are the only teacher in your school who is reading this book. Your colleagues are familiar with observations, but no one has heard of TDO before so they don't understand what makes it unique. If you decide to implement TDO in your classroom, you're going to need to recruit colleagues and explain to them the process structure and their roles. No one wants to sign up for something they don't understand (especially not extra observation time!), but as you discuss this with them, you can give them a vision of possibility.

To see how understanding plays directly into capability, consider this example. In a high school in Maine, one guidance counselor (of four) was significantly more effective at encouraging students to enroll in Advanced Placement classes. Her students were no more capable or motivated than others; rather, she simply framed the opportunity more effectively—describing what the experience was and was not. Because she created clarity for students, they began to participate and to succeed in something they hadn't thought was possible before.

Doing the same for your observers when you are the lead teacher will build their understanding of the process and their role within it. Communication is critical at these

A NOTE TO PRINCIPALS

Your communication is extremely important to the success of TDO in your school. Right off the bat, you should clearly communicate that TDO is not evaluative. By juxtaposing it against existing observation and evaluation models in the school, you can separate it from those other processes. When you help teachers see that the purpose of TDO is to collect data they request to help them improve their teaching, they will be better equipped to enter the process with an open mind and a productive disposition.

early stages of TDO, and particularly if you're initiating the process as an individual (rather than as a team or whole faculty). As in any other new process, the framing matters, particularly as you and your colleagues learn about the process. Accurately messaging the purpose of TDO can build interest, reduce anxiety, and encourage participation.

Key Point

In order to communicate the purpose of TDO effectively, the lead teacher must be clear about observers' roles, the objectives for the observation, the focus of the observation, and the method of data collection.

As the lead teacher communicating with your observers, it will be critical for you to clarify their roles for them (more on this topic later in this chapter) and take ownership of the process. When you clearly state your objective—to learn about a specific area of your instruction from the data they collect—you'll simultaneously be communicating the purpose of TDO. Identifying a clear focus for the observation, as well as selecting data collection methods for your observers to use (two topics we explore in depth in chapter 3), will ensure you get data that are important to you. It will also reinforce your role as leader and primary learner. The best opportunity to communicate the purpose and roles of TDO is as you begin—before misconceptions are built or, worse yet, put into practice.

THE TDO PROCESS

"Okay," Heather responds to Fernando. "Tell me more. How does it work?"

"Well, first you have a meeting where you prepare your observers by filling them in on what you're teaching and explaining your focus question. Then they come in for the observation at the time you designate. After, you guys meet for a short debriefing," Fernando explains.

"So this whole process revolves around me and my growth. I get it. I need to prepare well so I get the most out of it," says Heather.

As a teacher, you know from experience that any lesson you teach benefits from preparing beforehand and reviewing afterward. In the same way, a classroom observation by itself is not enough to transform teaching. Without a context for preparing for the observation and, even more important, discussing the implications of the data collected, it's unlikely that the observation will create long-term results. In order for TDO to be a powerful tool for professional learning, the observation needs to be flanked by a preobservation meeting and postobservation debriefing. If you follow each of the steps detailed below, you'll ensure that you, as the lead teacher, obtain data relevant to your focus area and then translate those data into instructional improvements:

- *Preobservation meeting.* This meeting serves as the opportunity for you to set the stage for the observation. Here you'll share with your observers your focus area—where you'd like to learn more in order to improve your instruction. You'll also briefly describe the context for the lesson and the logistics, including when the observation will occur and what data collection methods they'll employ. Your observers will have a chance to ask any lingering questions, equipping them with a clear purpose for the observation: to collect the data you want.

- *Observation.* The observation is the main event. It serves as the forum for collecting data in your classroom. Observers will arrive prepared to do what you asked them to do: script student dialogues or your questions, track your movement, describe student behavior, or collect details from one of many other data sources in your classroom. Observers will leave the observation with data in hand, ready to share this data with you in the postobservation debriefing.

- *Postobservation debriefing.* This final stage is the opportunity to share and examine the data. Guided by use of a protocol, you and your observers will analyze the data together. They'll share what they gathered during your lesson, and you'll have a chance to discuss the implications for instruction. Questions along the lines of, "So what?" and, ultimately, "Now what?" will be relevant as you commit to an instructional goal. This is the occasion that embodies the core of TDO: collected data become tangible resources for learning and instructional improvement.

It's tempting to take shortcuts—we know that time is one of the school resources in shortest supply. However, neglecting any of these steps is catastrophic to TDO. For instance, if you fail to take time to identify a focus and share it with your observers, the observation will be like shooting at a target with a blindfold on. Or if you choose not to schedule a debriefing meeting to share, examine, and discuss the data from the observation, you will not benefit from the collective experience and ideas of your colleagues. Both lead teachers and observers should understand that engaging in TDO is a three-part commitment, and each person's participation is critical at each step of the way.

TDO ROLES

In TDO, the observed teacher identifies the focus of the observation. The observers are data collectors who carefully record data for the observed teacher. These data, which the team will dig into collaboratively following the observation, serve as the source of learning for the observed teacher. This point is critical: in TDO, the primary learning value is for the observed teacher—a significant distinction from best-practice observation models where the observer leads the process or the evaluation model where the evaluator leads the process. While these differences among various observation models are simple on paper, they are dramatic in action.

For example, consider how Frank Bolton, a middle school science teacher, participates in an observer-led, evaluative observation. When he receives notification of the observation date and time, he prepares material and plans so that he can perform especially well during that time frame. When the day arrives, observers enter the room and note information that compares Frank against a teaching model with the goal of assessment. During the process, Frank might feel stressed, knowing that elements of his job could be affected by the outcome of this observation. When the observers finally gather their things and close the door, the whole room heaves a sigh of relief.

Let's look now at what's different when Frank participates in TDO. First, he takes time to reflect on an area where he'd like to improve his students' learning. With this focus, he develops a specific question, which he communicates in a pre-observation meeting to the colleagues he has selected as observers. He lets them know what data collection methods they should use to gather the information he

---

Key Point

A classroom observation by itself is not enough to transform teaching. Without a context for preparing for the observation and discussing the implications of the data collected, it's unlikely that the observation will lead to long-term results.

needs, and he answers any questions they have. When he opens his classroom door at the time they agreed on, he feels anticipation. Inviting them in, Frank teaches while the observers apply their eyes, ears, and experience to collect information that speaks to Frank's focus question. As they watch, Frank doesn't feel pressure to perform perfectly: he wants information about what really happens, not about what perfect performance might bring out in his students. After class, when his colleagues share the data they've gathered with him, he appreciates the added insight he now has about how his students learn.

Shifting the primary learning from the administrator or observer to the observed teacher has significant implications for the roles each participant adopts. For this reason, we clarify the purpose and the role of each participant in TDO.

A NOTE TO PRINCIPALS

To support lead teachers in their pivotal role, first structure opportunities for lead teachers to identify their focus areas. In one school, the principal set aside one hour during a professional development day for teachers to identify and develop a focus for their observation. This opportunity emphasized the importance of the lead teacher in taking charge of the process through identifying the focus of the observation. Second, you can emphasize that lead teachers are responsible for directing observers' attention and data collection methods. By reinforcing this, you clarify how the TDO process is different from other observation models.

Role of the Lead Teacher

Lead teachers are in the driver's seat for this ride. Each TDO participant gets a shot at being an observer and an observed teacher. When you're the lead teacher (or observed teacher), you are guiding the work. Your leadership role entails four primary tasks:

- Identifying a focus for the observation

- Engaging colleagues in the collection of classroom data

- Facilitating the conversations before and after the observation

- Using the data observers collect to inform your instruction

Through these four primary tasks, you'll set the tone for and direct the entire process. With that in mind, you can see why understanding this role is critical to creating an effective TDO experience for everyone. We'll discuss the lead teacher's role in more detail in later chapters, but for now, the most important thing to understand is that the lead teacher is guiding the observation process. When you understand this, your TDO experience can reach its potential as a source of meaningful, teacher-directed professional learning.

If the lead teacher misunderstands his or her role, the consequences translate directly into diminished outcomes. Consider what happens if the observed teacher fails to take the reins of the process, instead leaving the data collection process wide open. The likelihood that he receives relevant data or finds real value in the experience decreases significantly. Similarly, if the observed teacher fails to position herself as primary learner, she may erroneously assume that others are observing to develop their own skills rather than to help her develop her own. The result: she loses out on an opportunity for meaningful professional development.

Role of the Observers

Now let's switch gears. To highlight this role of observing teacher, let's look first at what observers often do in non-TDO types of classroom observations. In these observations, you might have freedom to observe whatever captures your interest. Your attention may be drawn to student conversations or to the student who sits quietly and works independently in the back corner of the classroom. You may take note of how the teacher redirects a student who misbehaves or examine the student work that covers one wall of the classroom. Perhaps the assignment the teacher gave students captures your interest, and you grab a copy to review as you sit at a back table. You have entered this classroom with the flexibility to direct your attention to whatever captures your interest. And that's precisely what happens: your attention goes to areas of *your* own interest. This may build your learning, but it does little to build the skills of the observed teacher.

Instead, in TDO, your role as an observer is to focus your attention vigilantly on the area the observed teacher has selected. Rather than recording a breadth of activities and information that may or may not directly inform the teacher's learning, you must narrow your attention to ensure you collect a depth of data, thereby equipping your team to engage in a robust postobservation conversation.

At its fundamental level, your role as an observer is that of data collector: you record and share data. Your role is not that of evaluator; you are not making meaning of or drawing conclusions about your observations while in the classroom. Instead you are scripting, describing, tracking, or counting what you see or hear. Thus, any teacher—new or veteran, inside or outside a content area—can be an effective observer.

Observers who fail to understand their role might arrive at the postobservation meeting with conclusions about effective or ineffective teaching, but without sufficient data to give the conversation context. It's easy to see how an observer who draws conclusions during the observation rather than collecting data will impede overall learning: participants are unable to analyze data if data have not been collected.

You may never have been in the role of the observer up to this point, but we predict that you'll grasp it quickly and jump into data collection with excitement. After all, if the observed teacher has been an effective leader of the process, you'll have a clear focus for your attention and straightforward methods for data collection. As you read the following chapters about what it takes to be an effective observer and data collector, you'll be empowered to enter a classroom with confidence that your attention is focused on the area that will most benefit the observed teacher.

Role of the Administrator

If you've read closely to this point, this section heading may have you asking, "What's the administrator got to do with this? I thought TDO is a teacher-led and teacher-focused process." You're right. Teacher-driven observation was created by and for teachers. That, however, doesn't exempt school administrators from participation in the process. They can be quite insightful observers and can help manage the logistics associated with TDO.

Fundamentally, TDO was created by and for teachers. However, school administrators can be insightful observers and helpful in managing logistics. You can guess that as a lead teacher, your observations and associated meetings require an investment of your time. An administrator can help you with resource allocation. We've seen administrators support TDO by providing professional development funds for release time and coverage by substitutes. Some eager administrators have even provided the class coverage themselves. With a view of the master

A NOTE TO PRINCIPALS

Do not dismiss the potential of your serving the role of a nonevaluative observer. In schools with strong trust between teachers and administrators, a principal can be a valuable observer. After all, principals have likely spent more time observing classrooms than most other people in the school. The perspective culled from these observations can be a valuable resource in the postobservation debriefing. Principals may have greater awareness of other teachers working on similar areas for improvement (thus they can connect teachers who may find a partnership helpful) or a wealth of ideas from their observations in other classrooms.

schedule, administrators can also offer assistance in grouping teachers who share common planning time.

No matter how an administrator may be involved within TDO, it's critical that she or he maintain a focus on TDO as a teacher-directed process. An administrator's involvement can instantly create confusion about the purpose of TDO—particularly if the administrator is also responsible for teacher evaluations. Thus, it's critical that any decision to involve administrators be intentional and in accordance with an existing environment of trust in a building.

FINAL THOUGHTS

If you know where you want to go, you'll have an idea of what you need to plan for along the way. Like the hiker preparing to experience the Appalachian Trail, knowing the purpose of your journey in TDO will clarify each phase of the process. Cultivating a strong understanding of your role in the process will help you navigate each element with ease—from distilling a focus question, to inviting colleagues, to conducting the postobservation debriefing.

Key Point

Fundamentally, TDO was created by and for teachers. However, school administrators can be insightful observers and helpful in managing logistics.

In the following chapter, we examine the first of the three steps of teacher-driven observation in detail. You'll see how to take charge in conducting a successful preobservation meeting, and we'll walk you through the process of creating a meaningful focus question. We also discuss choosing your team and resolving logistics. Having this information under your belt will equip you with the knowledge and skills to put these ideas into practice and to cultivate meaningful opportunities for professional development right in your classroom.

PART TWO

Implementing

Part One
Preparing

Part Two
Implementing

Part Three
Sustaining

CHAPTER THREE
THE PREOBSERVATION MEETING

H i, Jay! Are you free to come to my room for a fifteen-minute preobservation meeting right before school begins on Thursday morning?
Margaret said she could make that work, so I wanted to check in with
you. I promise to keep the meeting short so you can get to class on time! Send me
an e-mail when you get a minute. Thanks!" Heather finishes typing. She's scheduled her preobservation meeting for three days from now and knows she has a
bit of preparation to do. First, she's got to figure out her focus question. She can
still hear Fernando's advice ringing in her mind: "The more specific, the better!"
She pulls out a clean sheet of paper and writes at the top: "What I'd really like
to know about my teaching and my students." Her list gets more detailed as the
minutes pass.

It happens in locker rooms across the country. Sometimes the voices are loud
and sharp; other times there is earnestness, singing, even prayer. Before the big
game, athletes and coaches gather for a pregame meeting. Sometimes this event
looks like a huddle or a pep talk; usually it focuses on clarifying strategy toward
a common goal. People walk into this meeting as individuals but walk out united
as a team, ready to play full force toward achieving their goal. Collaborative
ventures of any sort—in boardrooms, on sports fields, or in school buildings—are
set up for success when all parties engage not only in the "main event" but also
in the preparation that occurs prior to the event. Just as coaches assemble their
team prior to each game, lead teachers invite their peers into their classroom
for their own pregame assembly: the preobservation meeting. These pregame
meetings share the same objective: to clarify the focus for the main event and
outline roles.

Teacher-driven observation (TDO) is a collaborative form of professional
development that is situated in the classroom and is teacher led from start to finish.

As the observed teacher, you take charge. You bear responsibility for leading this voyage, requesting the collection of data that will help you improve your teaching, and ultimately committing to tangible improvements that you can implement to support student learning. That's why you are called the "lead" teacher. It all starts with the preobservation meeting. As you read on, you can expect to generate ideas that are specific to your classroom and your own preobservation meeting.

In this chapter, we've assembled all the tools you need to create a successful preobservation meeting. First, we describe the purpose of the meeting so you have a clear sense of how it directly helps you accomplish your goals. Then we help you create a detailed focus question and select a method of data collection that will help your colleagues gather exactly the information you need to answer that question. We also help you think through which peers you'd like to invite to do your observation. Schedules can be busy for teachers, so we've compiled some useful suggestions for coordinating everyone's time in the observation process. We've also provided a list of common missteps to guide you through a successful TDO experience.

THE PURPOSE OF THE PREOBSERVATION MEETING

The preobservation meeting is arguably as important as the observation itself in that it sets the stage for the observation, providing all parties with a clear idea of what you, the observed teacher, hope to accomplish. This meeting takes you out of a passive role and places you at the helm of the process.

The preobservation meeting has three components (figure 3.1). First, you articulate your focus question. Without this integral step, observers would enter your classroom without a focused lens, ill prepared to collect data that inform your teaching and improve the learning that is taking place in your classroom. Second, you present the context for the lesson to your observers, who may be unfamiliar with the content you are teaching. Third, you and your team agree on logistical details for the observation and the postobservation debrief. In short, the preobservation meeting ensures that all participants are prepared to contribute.

Key Point

The preobservation meeting is arguably as important as the observation itself. This meeting provides all parties with a clear idea of what the lead teacher hopes to accomplish in the process.

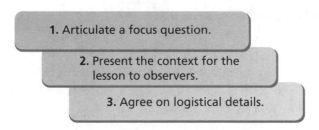

1. Articulate a focus question.

2. Present the context for the lesson to observers.

3. Agree on logistical details.

FIGURE 3.1. Components of the Preobservation Meeting

PREPARING FOR THE PREOBSERVATION MEETING

As any educator knows, when it comes to pulling off a plan, the devil is in the details. In the case of TDO, this couldn't be truer. To maximize your effectiveness, you must identify your focus for the observation and nail down the logistics.

Failing to identify and share your focus with observers is akin to enlisting the help of a Realtor in house shopping without having first defined the criteria you are looking for in a new home. The Realtor is likely to take you to homes that reflect her own interests rather than your own. Without a narrow focus, TDO will produce mediocre results at best. You will not get data that you seek and will be unable to gain insight that will lead to improvements in teaching and learning in your classroom. Simply put, if you don't name a focus, how can you expect your colleagues to collect relevant data?

Identifying a Focus Question

At its fundamental level, becoming a transparent teacher through TDO is about deciding what you want to learn. Selecting a focus question for your observation is your opportunity to articulate the area for this learning. As the leader of this process, you are best equipped to create a question that probes into the relationship between your instruction and student learning. While you may be tempted to identify several focus questions, you should select only one for the purpose of TDO. This ensures that your observers collect focused and relevant data in your classroom. If you try to answer multiple focus questions in a single observation, you risk answering none of them well.

Because our answers can be only as good as the question we ask, it's worth putting some effort into creating a pertinent, narrowed focus question. We can say this all day long, but that won't necessarily help you do it. So let's walk through the process together.

You already know the goal of the focus question: to learn something specific from data collection about the relationship between your instruction and student learning. Now we'd like you to imagine you are a fly. (Trust us on this one. Besides, at some level, haven't you wondered what it would be like to watch what goes on in your classroom?) Just become a fly and find an imaginary perch on the wall of your own classroom.

You now have a new vantage point. You have access to your blind spots—areas you either aren't or can't be aware of while you teach. Teaching takes a lot of concentration. But from this new (albeit imaginary) perspective, what might you see? What questions come to you? Jot down your ideas now, and we'll continue. For more detail, let's zoom in.

Key Point

As lead teacher, you may be tempted to identify more than one focus question. Remember that selecting a single focus question ensures that the data collected will answer the question.

Key Point

The goal of the focus question is to learn something specific about the relationship between your instruction and student learning through data collection.

First zoom your attention onto you as a teacher. Watch how you walk around the room. Listen to what you say and how you respond to student questions. Become aware of moments in the lesson when you're implementing the new strategy you learned last month in professional development. From this vantage point, how's it going? What would you like more information about? These areas could highlight potential blind spots that data could illuminate. Effective focus questions related to instruction might be, "How can I more effectively use reading workshop as an opportunity for students to interact with text?" or, "To what extent am I scaffolding the higher-level thinking questions I ask my students?" Even if you haven't perfected the wording, write down your thoughts right now about any areas where you'd like to have more information.

Next, zoom your attention onto your students. How well are they getting what you're saying? Watch where their eyes look as you're speaking, and listen to the comments they make. When do they zone out? You're already aware of many things as their teacher; for example, you know their test scores and their habits, so you don't need to look for this information in your focus question. As a fly on the wall, what things about your students can you see (or imagine) that you aren't aware of as you teach? Some helpful questions in this lens might be, "Which type of instructions best promote on-task cooperative group work, especially when I'm not hovering over a particular group?" or, "Am I using the gradual release of responsibility at a pace that promotes students' understanding of how to calculate molar mass?"

Write down any thoughts you discovered in terms of things you'd like to know about your students. Don't worry if your questions aren't as refined as the examples we listed; you'll get there. For now, just write. The beauty of observation is that its goal is to collect data on a question you care about, and data illuminate blind spots.

A NOTE TO PRINCIPALS

You can support teachers in selecting a focus area by providing resources such as those listed in table 3.1. Demonstrating your own openness and willingness to improve can model this process for teachers as well. In addition, you can offer example focus questions or opportunities for teachers to collaborate in creating focus questions.

If you're still working to come up with a focus question, table 3.1 lists some key resources that focus on teaching and learning strategies. In fact, if you haven't come up with a focus question about an existing need like the examples we just provided, you could create a new need by trying out a new strategy from one of the resources in the table.

The focus question you select should be one you cannot answer on your own; rather, it should require the collection of data from classroom observation. Consider the difference between asking, "Are my students able to solve multistep word problems?" and, "How do the questions I ask in class scaffold students' understandings of the steps required to solve multistep word problems?" The first question can be examined alongside student work samples, whereas the second requires examining a teacher's questions alongside evidence of student understanding such as student dialogue or student steps toward mastery of an academic task. Your observers are a valuable resource; be sure that your focus question requires the collection of data you otherwise do not have access to in the midst of teaching a lesson.

TABLE 3.1   RESOURCES FOR RESEARCH-BASED TEACHING AND LEARNING STRATEGIES

Janet Allen, *Tools for Teaching Content Literacy* (Portland, ME: Stenhouse, 2004).

Ceri Dean, Elizabeth Hubbell, Howard Pitler, and B. J. Stone, *Classroom Instruction That Works*, 2nd ed. (Alexandria, VA: Association for Supervision and Curriculum Development, 2012).

Jon Hattie, *Visible Learning* (New York: Routledge, 2008).

Bill Honig, Linda Diamond, and Linda Gutlohn, *Teaching Reading Sourcebook* (Novato, CA: Arena Press, 2000).

Madeline Hunter, *Mastery Teaching* (Thousand Oaks, CA: Corwin, 2004).

Doug Lemov, *Teach Like a Champion* (San Francisco: Jossey-Bass, 2010).

Robert Marzano, *The Art and Science of Teaching* (Alexandria, VA: Association for Supervision and Curriculum Development, 2007).

Jon Saphier, Mary Ann Haley-Speca, and Robert Gower, *The Skillful Teacher*, 6th ed. (Acton, MA: Research for Better Teaching, 2008).

Key Point

The focus question a lead teacher selects should be one that he or she cannot answer alone.

Sometimes it's helpful to see how another person does it. Let's go back to Heather's story. Earlier in this chapter, we saw her schedule her preobservation meeting. At this point, she's creating a focus question that will help her teach her seventh-grade math students more effectively. Notice how the question she comes up with provides the essential context for data collection during her observation:

Heather's students have been learning to calculate the surface area of three-dimensional objects. Some of them get it, but others need a bit more guidance. She has been using the gradual release of responsibility to help them work these calculations independently, without her prompting. Her strategy involves teacher modeling ("I do"), shared engagement in the task ("We do"), and then student independence in task completion ("You do"). This is the space where things get a bit hazy for her because it doesn't seem to be working. Well, it works in class when the students are partnered, but less so when they get to their assessments. This seems like a good area to focus on during her observation.

In developing a focus question, Heather thinks back to her class yesterday after lunch. She was working to improve the "we do" stage of gradual release, when students take increasingly more responsibility for completing the task, and noted the challenge of the transition from "we do" to "you do." From the questions her students asked, she could tell that some were more prepared to move on than others were. Those who could independently apply the formulas didn't have questions at all, but those who were struggling sometimes didn't even know what questions to ask; she could see the look of confusion on their faces. At that point, she started posing guiding questions to help them get through the calculations.

Heather decides this would be a good place to have Margaret and Jay's input because it's something she can't quite see clearly on her own. She writes her detailed focus question on her paper: "How are my words and actions contributing to students' taking on responsibility for calculating the surface area of three-dimensional objects?" Reading through it, she smiles. Fernando would be pleased with that level of detail.

Selecting a Data Collection Method

Armed with a focus question, you must now define the methods your peers will use to collect data during the observation. Typically you will request that at least one of your observers collect data involving the teacher and another collect data involving the students. This enables you to collectively examine the relationship between instruction and student learning in the postobservation debriefing. Although there are many ways observers can collect data, the most common methods are listed in table 3.2. We discuss the use of these methods in more detail in chapter 4.

Each focus requires the collection of different data. The following examples illustrate how lead teachers may link their focus areas to the collection of relevant data:

- A middle school physical education teacher wants to learn how she can more effectively group students to encourage student participation in class. She poses this question to her colleagues: "Which grouping strategies best contribute to student participation?" She requests that observers each observe one group of students and use the method of scripting to record how students in that group participate in the class activity, providing data that will inform her future grouping strategies.

- A ninth-grade algebra teacher wants to increase classroom engagement, particularly as it relates to students' participation in class discussions. Having recently implemented the strategy of cold calling, the teacher wants to know how he can more effectively frame questions so that they are accessible to all students. He asks his observers, "Am I providing adequate context for the questions I ask when I cold-call?" He requests that the observers script his questions and students' responses, providing him with a better understanding

TABLE 3.2 METHODS OF DATA COLLECTION

Method of Collection	Results: Data Collected
Scripting	Teacher instructions Teacher questions Teacher one-on-one conversations with students Student questions Student responses, categorized by: • Student volunteers • Student responds when called on • Student initiates a comment or question related to lesson • Student initiates an unrelated comment or question Student answers, categorized by: • Single word or phrase with no additional detail or support • Answer with details to support answer • Answer with explanation of thinking or processing used to develop answer Student side conversations
Counting	Teacher questions, categorized along Bloom's taxonomy Student questions Teacher instructional time Student work time Number of students who are on task Instances of specific student behaviors
Tracking	Teacher movements Teacher eye contact Student movements Student attention Group dynamics

of when students get confused. These data will help him scaffold these questions to encourage whole class participation and engagement.

Due to the sheer volume of data in a classroom, from dialogue to task to attention, many data sources could inform an answer to your focus question. Just as your question narrows the critical context of the observation, your data collection method will direct attention on that area. Let's examine how Heather identifies a relevant data collection method:

> Heather rereads her focus question, looking for what data her observers could collect to shed light on the issue: *How are my words and actions contributing to students' taking on responsibility for calculating the surface area of three-dimensional objects?* She knows how Jay and Margaret could collect many data from sources while they're in her room. They could script student conversations or describe the tasks in which students engage. They could record how she moves in the room and how that affects student attention.
>
> In the context of her lesson and her goal, Heather decides to have them collect data on the questions she asks and the questions her students ask. This information, she believes, will illustrate the distribution of responsibility for the academic task in her classroom. It'll shed light on her broad concern: Is she leading the learning, or are her students doing this? She decides to have Margaret script the questions she asks students (and count the total) and Jay script student questions (and count the total). Under her focus question, she writes, "Data collection methods: Scripting and counting." She's confident that these data will help her answer her focus question and, more important, improve her instruction.

At this point, we'd like you to look at the focus area you came up with and glance back at table 3.2. Write down which data sources and data collection methods seem most relevant for your question. If you want further information on data collection methods, read on. We go into each of these in greater detail in chapter 4. You should recognize that there's no right answer in this process; each pairing of a focus question and data collection method will yield interesting results. You should use logic to decide which would be of most value to your question, your students, and your learning.

Determining Who Will Collect the Data: Inviting Peers

Now that you've identified the what and the how of data collection, it's time to identify peers who will be most helpful in collecting the data you need. While this might seem like an easy task, it actually requires just as much thought as identifying what data observers will collect.

We recommend you invite between two and four peers into your classroom. Our experience has demonstrated that the collective insight of several teachers contributes to a more comprehensive data collection. The perspectives and expertise of the group is particularly relevant during the debriefing conversation when you are collectively making sense of the data and the implications for your classroom.

Each person in your building has had different experiences, resulting in a diversity of perspectives and insights that can support your efforts to improve your

TABLE 3.3 PROS AND CONS OF CATEGORIES OF PEER OBSERVERS

Categories of Observers	Pros	Cons
A peer who teaches many of the same students you do	Has knowledge of students' abilities	May have difficulty collecting unbiased data
A peer who works with an entirely different group of students	Has no knowledge of students' abilities that could potentially interfere with data collection	May have less understanding of your students' unique needs or strategies that have been effective with these students
A veteran teacher	Depth of experience; has had more experience to refine strategies and understand a context in which they are most effective	May be less familiar with new practices that have emerged in the field; has used practices for an extended period of time and thus may not remember the process of learning and refining them
A new teacher	May be closer to recent education research; hasn't yet established firm classroom routines so may be able to see other ways of doing things	Has less experience applying strategies to the classroom
A peer with deep knowledge of your subject area	Can better monitor students' understanding of classroom content; familiarity with instructional strategies as they relate to content	Curse of knowledge: it's harder for these observers to put themselves in the role of learner
A peer with little or no knowledge of your subject area	Able to see past content and instead look at instructional strategies; may have a lens that allows them to see new ways of teaching content	May have a harder time assessing student understanding
A teacher of a lower grade level	Has knowledge of what students should enter into higher grade knowing; may offer insight into why students with lower levels of ability are struggling with content	May not have knowledge of what students should know and be able to do
A teacher of a higher grade level	Can offer insight into what students will need to be able to do in upcoming grade levels; may offer insight into how higher-functioning students could be more challenged	May not have knowledge of what students should know and be able to do

instruction. Incredibly experienced and effective teachers can leverage their peers to improve—even when those peers are less experienced. Therefore, identifying which colleagues you will ask to engage with you in this process will require some thought about what insights specific individuals bring to the table. In table 3.3, we detail several common peer categories, along with the corresponding pros and cons.

Key Point

Teacher-driven observation is most beneficial when the lead teacher seeks out and invites a diverse group of peers who both share his or her desire to improve teaching practice and represent a wide range of backgrounds and experiences.

As you consider whom you will invite as observers into your classroom, we encourage you to think outside the comfort zones that exist in schools—most commonly, within grades or departments. Transparent teachers recognize that the colleagues with whom they have worked the least may in fact bring the greatest value to an observation. For example, at one school we witnessed a fifth-grade teacher inviting a third-grade teacher (among others) to observe in his classroom and collect data focusing on students' use of graphic organizers as a reading strategy. The third-grade teacher observed a small group of students struggling to use the strategy because of poor decoding skills. Her ability to notice this learning problem was due to the fact that she was commonly presented with this issue in her own classroom—an issue that the fifth-grade teacher had overlooked because his students had all entered his classroom as "readers."

Teacher-driven observation is the most beneficial for you and your observers if you seek out and invite a diverse group of peers who both share your desire to improve teaching practice and represent a wide range of backgrounds and experiences. Take a minute to write down a few names that come to mind as possible observers; feel free to refine this list as you read on. Teacher-driven observation is all about learning from your peers and the data that they collect while observing your practice. For this reason, you'll want to seek out and invite peers who have a sincere desire to learn along with you and are invested in the improvement that will result from this process. Our experiences have shown that it is from these individuals that you will be able to collect the most useful data to inform and improve your practice.

Ironing out the Logistics

As the lead teacher, you are in charge of planning for logistics. This means that you'll need to think through two elements carefully: details and scheduling. In terms of details, you'll want to walk into the preobservation meeting with a plan for the entire process: when the observation will take place, where your colleagues will stand or sit during the observation, how they'll interact with your students, and when and where the postobservation debriefing will take place.

Scheduling, perhaps the most complicated logistical matter to tackle, depends largely on you and your observers' availability. Because classroom observations pull several teachers away from their day-to-day schedules, you might need to get creative. For situations where common planning time does not exist, the preobservation meeting can be completed in as little as fifteen minutes—a time frame that can easily occur before school on the day of the observation or after school the day before the observation. You could also potentially schedule the meeting immediately before the observation (when your observers are available) by asking another colleague who has a planning period to cover your class for fifteen minutes while you lead the preobservation meeting. And of course everyone has to eat lunch; if your lunch periods overlap, you could use fifteen minutes of this shared time for your discussion. Although this list of suggestions is not exhaustive, we have seen teachers experience success at using these three scheduling techniques.

> ### A NOTE TO PRINCIPALS
>
> You can support teachers in planning the logistics for their observations. They may need assistance knowing which colleagues have planning time that overlaps their own, for example.

Take a moment and write down what timing seems to be most feasible for the observation. You might know already when the colleagues you selected are available, but if you don't, consider what timing would be best for you. There are ways to make this meeting happen without much inconvenience. In chapter 6, we discuss several creative ideas. As the leader in TDO, your preparation for the preobservation meeting has a direct effect on the overall outcome. Your peers will find value in being part of a focused process that is designed to improve teaching and learning. By ironing out the logistics, you are setting up yourself and your peers for success.

A PREOBSERVATION MEETING IN ACTION

Having prepared for the preobservation meeting, you are now ready to open your doors and invite your peers to engage in TDO. We will continue following Heather as she prepares for and conducts her preobservation meeting. Her experiences illustrate how preparation builds the capacity of all involved to contribute meaningfully to the observation process.

On the morning of the observation, Heather arranges a circle of three chairs at the back of her classroom, and, as planned, the preobservation meeting starts promptly at 7:45 a.m. She's feeling confident in her ability to equip Margaret and Jay with the information they need to collect relevant data, building their capacity as observers. Heather greets her colleagues and hands each a copy of the preobservation protocol (see figure 3.2). "I promised we'd be brief! This protocol will structure our conversation and ensure that we finish the meeting in the fifteen minutes available before the school day begins," she says.

FIGURE 3.2. Protocol for the Preobservation Meeting

Facilitator (teacher being observed): Heather

Focus question: How are my words and actions contributing to students taking on responsibility for calculating the surface area of three-dimensional objects?

Protocol

1. Lead teacher provides logistical information for both observation and postobservation debriefing. (2 minutes)

   - Observers ask clarifying questions. (1 minute)

2. Lead teacher provides the context for the lesson and shares the focus question. (3 minutes)

   - Observers ask clarifying questions. (2 minutes)

3. Lead teacher explains data collection templates and assigns roles for collecting data. (3 minutes)

   - Observers ask clarifying questions. (2 minutes)

Heather begins the meeting: "You'll be observing my seventh-grade math class, which meets during period 3. It'll be most helpful to me if you can come to my classroom from 10:00 to 10:20. As a reminder, we agreed to meet here in my room to debrief as soon as school lets out. If we start right on time, we'll be done by 3:15. Before I describe the context of my lesson, do either of you have any questions about logistics?"

"So, we don't need to be in your classroom for the whole period—only the time you identified?" Jay inquires.

"Right—just that twenty minutes. Of course, you're welcome to come earlier or stay later, but I know your time is valuable, and I'm also confident you'll be able to collect plenty of data in that time frame."

Next, Heather gives her colleagues a one-minute summary of the unit she is teaching on calculating the surface area of three-dimensional objects. She also outlines the strategy she's implementing: "You'll recall that the gradual release method is the 'I do, we do, you do' strategy. Earlier this week, I modeled how to calculate surface area of three-dimensional objects, and yesterday we did several examples as a whole class. Gradual release can be a powerful process for supporting student learning, but as you know, I'm not able to fully assess how effectively I'm implementing the strategy while I'm teaching. I'm particularly interested in what works well and what doesn't work as I release responsibility to students. That's where you come in." She pauses and both nod, following her reasoning.

"Of course, the additional challenge is that some students are ready to do the math independently, and others need more collective practice. During the time you'll be in my room, I'll be releasing responsibility to the students—asking them to solve problems in small groups and then coming back together as a class to review their work. What questions do you have for me at this point?" Heather asks.

"You likely have already thought of this, but I'm wondering how you might release responsibility at different paces for different learners," Margaret asks.

"Great question, Margaret. It's been on my mind as well. I have been structuring my questions to speak to different learners, but that's something I'm hoping you can watch for in my class today. We should revisit this idea when we debrief this afternoon.

"No questions, Jay? Okay. Well, my focus question for this observation is: 'How are my words and actions contributing to students taking on responsibility for calculating the surface area of three-dimensional objects?' I'm hoping that this question will focus your attention during the time you're in my class.

"Sometimes I find it difficult to step back. It will be particularly helpful for me, Margaret, if you will script the questions I am asking my students so I can examine how I am releasing responsibility. I'd also like to have data on the questions my students ask so I can see to what extent they are taking responsibility for the task. Jay, will you script the student questions? Also, would each of you tally up the total of the questions you script? Those numbers could come in handy. Thanks!"

Heather passes out the data collection forms (see figure 3.3): "Here's a template you can use to record the data. I've created this template so that you'll have all the information that you need in one place. It includes my focus question as well as the method of data collection that you'll be using. Any questions?"

FIGURE 3.3. Data Collection Template

Grade level observed: Seventh grade

Subject: Math

Date: November 6

Focus question: How are my words and actions contributing to students taking on responsibility for calculating the surface area of three-dimensional objects?

Data collection method: Scripting and counting

Note: To download a blank version of this data collection template for your own use, go to www.eddirection.com/templates.

Jay nods, "When I script student questions, do you want me to also record which student asked the question?"

Heather responds: "That could be quite helpful, particularly because you already know these kids from your social studies class. Any other questions? No? Well, I'm really looking forward to having you help me collect this data! Thank you for your time. I'll see you today during third period, and we'll meet here again at 3:00 for the debriefing."

COMMON MISSTEPS

The success of TDO depends largely on the thoughtfulness and intentionality of the planning that precedes the observation itself. To help you steer clear of avoidable hiccups and take charge of your observation, here are some of the most common missteps we have seen in preparing for TDO.

Key Point

The success of TDO depends largely on the thoughtfulness and intentionality of the planning that precedes the observation itself.

Neglecting to Prepare for the Preobservation Meeting

You get out of this meeting what you put into it. If you shortchange your preparation time in identifying a focus question or selecting data collection methods, you shortchange your results. Both you and your colleagues benefit greatly when you take the time to plan details and logistics. With clarity in these areas, you can be confident that TDO will provide you with a wealth of knowledge about your teaching and student learning.

Choosing a Superficial Focus Question

Superficial focus questions—ones you've already answered or that concentrate on topics tangential to student learning—undermine your ability to leverage TDO as an opportunity for learning. As long as your focus question can be answered with observable data and is grounded in an area that is important to teaching and learning, you're on the right track to having a meaningful TDO experience.

Not Taking the Lead

As the lead teacher, you are responsible for driving the TDO process. Teachers experienced in the process of TDO know they can blame only themselves if they fail to reap learning from the process. By stepping up to lead this process, you are taking the proverbial bull by the horns and ensuring that this process provides meaningful insight into your daily instruction.

Approaching Teacher-Driven Observation as a "Model Classroom" Observation Process

TDO is not about finding "model classrooms" or finding an "expert" teacher and asking for feedback on how you can become an expert. Success in TDO depends on your willingness to engage with your peers in collecting data. We encourage you to consider the knowledge and skills that each of your colleagues can bring to the table.

> ### Key Point
>
> *TDO is not about finding "model classrooms" or finding an "expert" teacher and asking for feedback on how you can become an expert.*

Failing to Open Yourself Up to Improvement

Going through the motions of TDO without truly opening yourself up to feedback and learning will result in a loss of precious time. Committing to being open to improvement, even when you feel vulnerable, is the first step in becoming a transparent teacher.

FINAL THOUGHTS

In a world of private practice, opening your classroom door requires much more than having observers sit in your classroom as you teach your students. Successfully taking charge demands thought and preparation, a process that begins long before you find yourself teaching a lesson as your peers observe and collect data. The preobservation meeting is the first stage in opening your door: it's the pregame meeting where you equip your peers with the focus they need to collaboratively offer valuable insight into your teaching and learning.

In the next chapter, we jump into the observation. We discuss in greater detail the three main data collection methods so you can choose which one (or more) you'd like to have your observers leverage on your behalf. We also explore the role of the observer and offer tips for getting the most out of the observation day.

CHAPTER FOUR
THE OBSERVATION

Margaret could hear the steady hum of student conversation inside Heather's classroom and chairs squeaking against tile floor as students pushed back from their desks. She smiled, recognizing the familiar sound: her students did that all the time. Margaret pulled a pen and the data collection template from her bag as she prepared to enter the classroom to observe her colleague. She knew the data her team would gather would make a difference, but she wondered how the experience would play out. Teachers in her school regularly encouraged each other but always stayed on their own turf.

The chatter hushed as Margaret heard Heather delivering instructions and turning the door handle. Entering the room as an observer, Margaret felt as if she was crossing a long-established teaching boundary.

PURPOSE OF THE OBSERVATION

When you open your classroom door and invite your colleagues in to collect data, you replace isolation with connection. You learn about and refine your practice in a way that is nearly impossible to do in a professional development session located outside your classroom. When you engage in conversations with your colleagues about the context of student learning and in the context of your own classrooms, you become a transparent teacher taking charge of your own professional development.

Key Point

In teacher-driven observation, being an observer means being a data collector. Observers focus on gathering data that the lead teacher has requested.

The best way to examine instruction is to stand in a classroom and watch it happen. Real-time action always trumps theory. No book, training session, or instructional video has the capacity to illustrate the complex learning processes or the nuances of human interactions in classrooms in the way that classroom observation can. Do you recall the last time you were in a professional development session and learned a new teaching strategy? As you considered implementing the strategy in your classroom, it seemed simple. But when you tried it, the difference between sitting in the session and standing in the classroom became apparent because teaching is a hands-on endeavor. Learning in classrooms minimizes the transfer that traditional professional development sessions require. Put another way, the best way you can ensure that the strategies you're learning actually work with your students in your classroom is by doing your professional learning right in your classroom with your students.

Contrary to student lore, you do not have eyes in the back of your head. You're busy making connections, asking questions, and delivering content, so you don't consciously notice how many students ask questions or how your movements in the room affect student participation. You cannot possibly be aware of the dialogue that passes between students in group sessions because there's just too much going on.

Fortunately, schools come ready-made with reinforcements: your colleagues can put their eyes, ears, and experience to work for you in your classroom. When they step in to observe, you benefit from their capacity to collect data in real time.

THE INSTRUCTIONAL CORE

What occurs in the classroom powerfully illustrates the intersection of student, teacher, and content. When you stand in others' classrooms as an observer, you can watch how these three elements of the instructional core[1] interact with each other and how they affect teaching and learning (see figure 4.1). All too often, opportunities for professional learning focus on only one aspect of the instructional core—perhaps the strategies or materials you use. This approach, however, has a glaring shortcoming: it bypasses the fact that effective teachers

Key Point

Professional learning opportunities often focus on only one aspect of the instructional core, an approach that has a major flaw: it bypasses the fact that effective teachers choose strategies and materials for communicating content in real-time response to student learning needs.

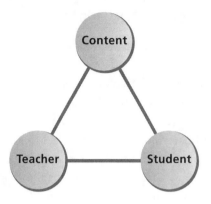

FIGURE 4.1.   The Instructional Core

choose strategies and materials for communicating content in real-time response to student learning needs.

For instance, many teachers spend hundreds of hours in professional development sessions and department meetings where they discuss isolated pieces of the instructional core—from primary sources in a World War I unit (content) to the merits of wait time (teacher) to student behavior (student). Analyzing all three components of the instructional core at the same time is essential to making classroom improvements because it's only then that we'll understand the essential relationships that exist among them.

A NOTE TO PRINCIPALS

Send a clear message in your meetings and activities that all school efforts are focused on the instructional core.

Observation removes the guesswork. It delivers concrete answers about how teachers and students work with content. When teachers have observation data from their classrooms to guide their professional learning, they can review specific detail about how students reacted to a primary source document and which sources seemed to have the greatest impact on learning. What's more, conversations and decisions grounded in data remove preconceptions about kids and content. You stop talking about what you think might happen and begin examining what actually occurred and how well it worked. Observation data, then, inform your ability to harmonize the multiple components of the instructional core effectively in your classroom.

METHODS OF DATA COLLECTION

As the lead teacher, you are in charge of the observation that occurs in your classroom: you decide the focus, invite observers, and select data collection techniques. These data collection techniques offer unique insight into how the instructional core elements are interacting at, say, 10:08 on Tuesday morning in your classroom. Because the core elements are always working in relation to each other, what happens in one class won't be what happens in the next, but each instance is valuable for data collection. In chapter 3, we briefly addressed data collection techniques; in this chapter, we explore these methods in more detail, illustrating how they zoom in on particular elements of the instructional core and thereby create the foundation for a meaningful postobservation dialogue.

The resources we present here are not exhaustive, but we predict you'll see a variety of methods that you can enlist to collect data in your classroom. Most important, the method you select should be specific to the question you're studying in this round of teacher-driven observation (TDO). You can and should employ different methods to answer different questions or even to study different aspects of the same focus area. Having a specific data collection method provides clarity and direction for your observers: they'll know where to focus their attention and will have the capacity to deliver relevant data to you in the postobservation debriefing. If you have questions about which data collection method you should use for your focus question, we recommend you consult your colleagues prior to the preobservation meeting.

In this chapter, we explore three specific data collection methods: scripting, counting, and tracking. Each of these can be relevant when gathering teacher or student data. We examine their benefits and limitations and illustrate them in classroom scenarios for primary and secondary schools. You may see elements of these situations that apply to your school and classroom. We also look at the role of observers as they use these collection methods and discuss common missteps.

Student Data Versus Teacher Data

One of the most critical decisions you make regarding data collection methodology is whether to have your observers collect teacher data, student data, or both. Often teachers engaged in TDO request that observers collect both student and teacher data, because the two together can more fully illustrate the relationship between teaching and student learning. For example, if you want to understand the effects of wait time on student participation, you need to examine data on both the periods of wait time you provide students to think before they respond to a question (two seconds or ten?), and on how students respond when given this wait time (Do their answers seem robust? Are many students prepared to respond?).

There's another factor for consideration when you're deciding whether to collect teacher data, student data, or both. If you've been observed only for purposes of evaluation, you might feel a bit anxious starting out with TDO. If this applies to you, you might choose to have your observers collect student data during the first observation so the observers' attention will be focused more on students than on you until you are comfortable with the process.

Sometimes you'll choose to have observers focus only on collecting teacher data. This can come in handy when you really want to tackle data-based answers to how your actions, words, and movements are affecting the class. If you ask observers to focus only on you, their data will draw for you a picture of where you were in the classroom, what you said, and what you did. These details, in combination with each other, are often invisible to us while we're teaching—we just walk and talk without thinking about our collective actions.

Because TDO highlights the instructional core in action, we predict you'll find the greatest benefits from assigning observers to collect both student and teacher data, particularly as you become more familiar with TDO. Be intentional in your decision, weighing the benefits and limitations of the various data collection methods, and you'll create success in your observation.

Scripting Methods

From teacher instructions to small group student conversations, scripting methods can capture a wealth of data in the classroom. In scripting, the observer transcribes interactions among students and between students and the teacher. The detail inherent in scripted data can provide insight into student thinking that counting and tracking methods cannot capture. As an example, let's look at one difference between counting data and scripting data: whereas counting data communicates that two students asked a question at the end of a lesson on calculating surface area of a cylinder, scripting data indicate what the questions were: "Well, now that we know how to calculate surface area, how do we calculate volume?" and, "How do we calculate the surface area of a sphere?" Certainly the transcriptions illustrate a level of student thinking that a counting method of data collection fails to capture.

Because scripting methods capture such a high level of detail, they can be relevant to nearly every focus area. You can see how this plays out in these examples:

- A fifth-grade teacher wants to improve her questioning strategy, so she creates this focus question: "How can I more effectively use questions to scaffold student learning?" Then she makes an effort to respond to their questions with her own questions to prompt their thinking, particularly as students engage in group and independent math practice. For her observation, she invites two of her colleagues into her classroom and requests that they collect data on this focal area. She asks each one to sit with a small group of students and script the questions students ask and the questions she asks. These scripts show her how she responds to student learning needs through the use of questions.

- An eleventh-grade chemistry teacher is working to develop students' positive interdependence during lab experiments, hoping that students will come to rely on one another's knowledge in order to complete the lab. He splits the academic material into separate parts, giving individual parts to team members in order to foster this positive interdependence and creates this focus question: "How does the division of materials contribute to positive interdependence in lab groups?" Inviting three of his colleagues into his classroom to collect data, he asks them to each sit with a group and script the students' comments and questions throughout the lab time. The data his observers collect enable him to analyze how the division of materials affects their positive interdependence.

Of course, scripting methods present their own challenges. Scripting is an intense assignment, particularly if an observer is tasked with scripting a teacher's instructions or entire student conversations. The pace of an energetic teacher or excited students can easily outpace even the most adept scribe. Narrowing the focus for scripting can help address this challenge. An observer may record only students' responses to questions or only conversations between the teacher and individual students. A team of observers can come in handy here as well: one observer scribes a teacher's questions while another scribes students' responses.

And although scripted data undoubtedly provide a valuable level of detail—whether it is student understanding, as evident in responses to questions, or the collaborative dynamics of student groups—this level of detail can inhibit broader analysis of classroom-wide dynamics. The student questions illustrated in the math example might provide insight into students' curiosities about additional applications of their math skills but not into the remaining learning needs of other students in the class. Counting and tracking data collection methods can complement the data collected through scripting.

Counting Methods

The sheer number of students in classrooms today makes counting a feasible way to collect data on many students simultaneously. On the surface, counting methods can appear rather bland as a data collection tool, particularly alongside the richness of scripted data. However, counting methods are valuable in providing a comprehensive view of classroom patterns. Through counting methods, you can examine the distribution of classroom time, the percentage of students who are on task (which requires a description about what "on task" looks like exactly), or the number of questions you ask that are at each level of Bloom's taxonomy. These numbers can serve as a starting point for rich debriefing conversations. The following examples illustrate counting methods in action:

- A fourth-grade teacher wants to analyze the efficacy of small reading groups. She believes in the value of allocating time for the students to read and has been using homogeneous groupings and differentiated, level-appropriate texts to encourage readers of all skill levels to read aloud and think critically about the text. She intends for this strategy to increase on-task time for both the above- and below-grade-level readers. Her focus question is: "How does the use of homogeneous groupings and differentiated level-appropriate texts contribute to keeping readers on task?" During the observation, the teacher asks one observer to sit with the above-level group and the other with the below-grade-level group. She asks them to count the number of comments each student makes, as well as the number of times a student demonstrates behavior that shows poor attention—such as putting the book down, not turning the page in time, or focusing attention away from the book or conversation. With these counts, she will have a concrete sense of how well students are staying on task in their groups and how effective the reading groups are.

- A high school music teacher has been focusing on increasing the amount of class time during which students are playing their instruments. He knows this factor is critical to the development of their skills and wants to learn more about the distribution of time in his orchestra class. His focus question is: "How can I increase my students' playing time during class?" To answer that question, he needs to know how much the students are currently playing in class so he can find ways to increase it. Therefore, he requests that each of his observers sit with a section of students and record the time throughout his fifty-five-minute class period that students are playing their instruments. Observers use stopwatches to count the number of minutes students are playing, as well as the number of minutes the teacher is providing direct instruction. With the concrete numbers that come from this counting method, he will have a clear sense for how much time his students are playing, and he'll be able to make changes where necessary.

Although counting methods provide a broad view of a pattern in a classroom, they lack the ability to illustrate the teaching and learning within a pattern. For this reason, counting can really become powerful in combination with scripting or tracking. We'll discuss this idea further as we look at using multiple methods, but at this point, let's look at a strong example of what can happen in a classroom when observers use both counting and scripting.

Return with us to Heather's observation day in her seventh-grade math class. As you recall from the previous chapter, she decided to focus on how her words and actions helped her release responsibility to her students for calculating the surface area of various three-dimensional shapes. She asked one observer, Margaret, to both script and count the questions she posed. Heather knew that the data Margaret gathered would give her a concrete list of how many questions she was asking and what their content included. Responding to her students' questions would take enough of Heather's concentration that she was grateful for Margaret's eyes and ears in gathering this information. To get a broader sense of how her questions affected her students, the instructional core interplay on this issue, she asked the other observer, Jay, to script and count the questions that her students asked.

Heather's choice to combine counting with scripting allowed her observers to collect data that were relevant to her focus area: seeing how her words—what she asked and how often she questioned students—made a difference in releasing responsibility to her students for their calculations. While it's hard to quantify or count how well the release of responsibility is working, the results become evident in her students' words and actions. If the questions Jay scripts from the students are few and show that students have a solid understanding of the process, Heather will know that they are getting the hang of calculating the surface area of various three-dimensional shapes. If instead they ask many questions that demonstrate confusion, Heather will know she has some work to do toward releasing responsibility and enabling them. If Heather had requested the data collection method of counting alone for her observation, she would end up knowing that she asked, say, twelve questions while her students asked fifteen. That gives her some information to work with, but by including scripting with counting, Heather will have a record of what those questions were about.

In the next chapter, you'll find out what Heather's observers recorded and how she had an important breakthrough because of what she discovered. For now, it's important to note that her breakthrough came because she employed the combination of scripting and counting. Multiple methods of data collection shine light on multiple facets of the focus question, and counting makes a particularly useful adjunct for the scripting and tracking.

Tracking Methods

Have you ever wondered how your physical location in the classroom affects the way your students learn? What if you could quantify how well your nonverbal cues worked to redirect student behavior? Like counting, tracking data collection methods can help illustrate patterns that exist in a classroom. As with counting and scripting, tracking methods can focus on the teacher or the students, or on both. Because we are often unaware of our movement or the way we direct our attention while we teach, this information can be illuminating.

Tracking classroom data can involve recording the movement of a teacher—during a lecture, cooperative student group work, or independent student practice—in order to examine student attention or group dynamics. Heather was curious about how her words and her actions affected her students. In a future observation, she could ask her colleagues to gather tracking data, and she would get added insight. Observers can also track students' movements, data that can be relevant in examining classroom transitions or cooperative learning activities. For instance, if an observer records that a student got out of her seat five times in twenty minutes, the teacher will be able to evaluate what he's doing to address that or to engage this student's attention. In addition to movement, tracking methods can capture eye contact and attention. These data can provide the context for inquiry into the effects of nonverbal cues on student behavior or the distribution of attention (through eye contact) during a class period.

The following examples illustrate tracking data collection methods in the context of TDO:

- A first-year third-grade teacher is working to improve the efficiency of his stations. He has noticed that several students tend to wander between stations, and many are not able to complete a station's activity in an appropriate amount of time. He has a hunch that students are struggling to understand the purpose of each station, which affects their motivation to dive into each one. His focus question is therefore, "How do my students' understanding of the purpose of their station activities influence their participation in each station?" In order to understand better the flow of traffic, he asks one observer to track the path that all students from two specific groups take across and within each station. Then he tasks two other observers with asking purpose questions of both wandering and on-task students: "Why are you doing stations today?" and, "What is the purpose of this station?" The teacher hopes that the tracking data, as well as the answers from students, will yield insightful information about the extent of the wandering problem. He hopes that in the debriefing meeting, he and his colleagues can discuss how to help the wanderers be more on task.

- A ninth-grade social studies teacher wants to improve her classroom management, particularly in redirecting off-task students without interrupting the pace of the class. She has been implementing nonverbal cues to redirect students during direct instruction and affirm positive behavior. Her focus question is, "How well do my students change their behavior when I give them nonverbal cues?" Hoping to examine the balance of these positive and corrective nonverbal cues, she has one observer track these cues—from her eye contact to her facial expressions—and another observer track student attention in response to these cues. With these tracking data, she hopes to get a clear sense for how well her nonverbal cues are working to redirect students.

Tracking data collection methods illustrate the patterns—whether it's our movement or attention as teachers or the movement or attention of students—that are overshadowed by the demands of instruction on our attention. These patterns are often collected on a classroom seating chart, which provides a context for observers to easily record data as they draw arrows to track movement and attention. We've found that when a lead teacher provides her observers with a seating chart or classroom map, observers can more easily and accurately use tracking methods for data collection.

The simplicity of a seating chart filled with arrows documenting a teacher's movement throughout the class can be a powerful source of data. In fact, one of the benefits of using a tracking data collection method is that the data have power in their visual presentation: the data begin to speak for themselves, particularly if arrows are congregated in one part of the class. Of course, no classroom environment is as simple as a single data set, and the shortcoming of tracking methods is that when they are used in isolation, they fail to paint a comprehensive picture of the reasons behind classroom movement or attention.

Key Point

The top three TDO data collection methods are scripting, counting, and tracking. You can use each of these to collect student data, teacher data, or both.

Multiple Methods

As you're considering what method might be most appropriate to the focus question you generated, we recommend you consider using more than one. Although we've presented data collection methods by category, it is perhaps most helpful to think about the ways a variety of methods can complement one another. Each method offers its own specific value and challenges, which we've summarized in table 4.1. Using multiple methods can enable you to account for these and ensure the collection of robust data.

Let's say you are planning to collect data on cooperative learning in student groups. You might have one observer track conversation within a student group, noting the direction of conversation. Another observer could collect data on the length of time each student contributes to the group's dialogue. A third observer would script the conversation. Together these three data sets can provide you with a comprehensive picture to explore how students are using cooperative learning opportunities and how you can effectively structure this learning time.

THE ROLE OF THE OBSERVER

At some level, you might ask whether a camera could serve the role of the observer. Why should a person sit in the classroom scripting questions, counting instances of a behavior, or tracking movements? Certainly any footage, if it were properly focused, could broadly record that information. The reason it's so important to have your colleagues perform the observation is that they can offer insight that helps you draw conclusions. You have the benefit of their brainpower throughout the process, and they will discern things that you might not if you were to watch the situation unfold on camera. They also have the capacity as observers to sit with groups of students and interact with them.

The role of the observer is paramount during the observation. It is the observer who collects data—data that you would otherwise be unable to gather due to the multitude of demands pulling on your attention in the classroom. You can imagine the challenge of trying to script the questions you ask students while guiding a class discussion or the complexity of tracking your movement in the classroom

Key Point

Engaging other professionals in TDO is important. Unlike a camera recording the lesson, they can offer insight and help you, as lead teacher, draw conclusions.

TABLE 4.1   METHODS OF COLLECTING DATA

	About the Method	Examples	Challenges
Scripting	Observer transcribes interactions among students or between students and the teacher, or both Provides rich data about students' and teacher's actions, statements, and questions Can be relevant to most focus areas Can focus on teacher, student, or both	Observer scripts all of the questions that students ask during lesson Observer scripts teacher's responses to students' questions Observer records a description of how students interact with one another during group time	Intensive task Can yield data that are focused on one element within the classroom, resulting in a narrow view of teaching and learning
Counting	Logical way to collect data on a large number of students Valuable in providing a comprehensive view of patterns occurring within the classroom Can focus on teacher, student, or both	Observer counts the number of minutes devoted to certain tasks Observer counts the number of questions asked and answered	When used on its own, method lacks the ability to illustrate what teaching and learning look like Is most useful when used in conjunction with other data collection methods
Tracking	Helps illustrate patterns occurring within a classroom Can focus on teacher, student, or both	Observer tracks teacher's movements throughout the classroom during instruction Observer tracks students' movements from one learning area to another during the lesson	Can fail to provide a comprehensive look at teaching and learning when used in isolation Is most useful when used in conjunction with other data collection methods

as you're teaching. Teaching requires a level of focus that precludes such data collection. The role of the observer exists to do just that. For your observers to do their job well, you have to set the stage for your class so that your students aren't confused about what is going on.

STUDENT-OBSERVER INTERACTIONS

"Who's that?!" students typically whisper when a new adult enters a classroom. Their reactions can vary from excitement to curiosity to worry when there's a new face in the room. Some students may view the occasion as a time to disrupt the routine of the day. Others may feel anxiety that the adult is there to observe their own behavior. Most students are not used to visitors (or two or three of them) in their classroom, and the reality is that the new presence can become a distraction.

Deciding how to address this topic with students is ultimately your decision. Informing your students that visitors will be coming into the classroom can help reduce the distraction, particularly if students understand why the observers are there. One teacher used this occasion to highlight her role as a learner alongside her students by telling them, "Like you, I am always learning to develop my skills. The visitors we'll have later today are here to help me learn. I'm excited they'll be here with us because they'll collect information about my teaching that I'll be able to use to learn more about our classroom."

We've also found that students come to ignore the presence of observers when this practice becomes commonplace in a school. They soon discover that these adults do little to make the class more exciting. In one elementary school, several administrators intentionally visited classrooms more often as teachers began planning for the TDO process, increasing students' comfort with adult visitors.

In addition to clarifying the experience for your students, it's necessary to clarify the interactions—or lack of interactions—you expect your observers to have with your students. Sometimes, in order to capture the routine happenings in a classroom, you may request that your observers not interact with students at all. However, more often than not, you may find that these interactions can make important contributions to the data collection in your classroom. An observer's request to a student, "Tell me about what you're doing in class and why you're doing it," can provide access to a robust data source: student thinking and perception. As you decide whether to have your observers engage with your students, keep your focal area in mind.

COMMON MISSTEPS

Observers should watch out for the common pitfalls of losing focus on data collection, sacrificing objectivity to a personal lens, and making meaning rather than collecting data. You could look at this section inversely as tips for getting the most out of your observation day by making sure your observers collect data and stay objective.

Losing Focus on Data Collection

It's critical that observers hold their primary role at the forefront of their minds. Although we teachers are in the classroom daily, we seldom have the opportunity to observe our colleagues in action or watch students in a classroom other than our own.

As a result, we've found that one of the greatest challenges the observer faces is staying focused on the task at hand: collecting the data the lead teacher has requested. Armed with the task of scripting student conversations, observers sometimes find themselves ten minutes into an observation with little written down. This is not for lack of effort but simply because it is fascinating to listen to students engage in dialogue. It's also easy to be pulled into the content of the lesson and the energy of the classroom such that we forget briefly our role as an observer.

The danger with this behavior is that we lose focus on why we're in the classroom: to collect data for the lead teacher. Unlike observation models where the observers lead the process and hope to learn ideas from the observation, TDO positions the observed teacher as the leader of the process. And while you will certainly pick up new ideas and learn about instruction from being an observer, it's critical that this does not overshadow your primary responsibility as an observer: to record data.

> **Key Point**
>
> *Observers should be aware of three common pitfalls: losing focus on data collection, sacrificing objectivity to a personal lens, and making meaning rather than collecting data.*

> ## A NOTE TO PRINCIPALS
>
> You can support teachers in remaining focused on data collection during the observation, observing with objectivity, and avoiding making meaning of the data too early in the process. You can model this yourself as well as continue to remind observers in your school.

Sacrificing Objectivity to a Personal Lens

As observers, we also enter classrooms carrying our own experiences and perceptions—both of which influence the lens through which we observe our surroundings. Our own interests often direct our attention, even unconsciously. One of us has four young sons, a factor that has him most curious about the ways in which boys are engaged in reading and writing instruction. When he enters an elementary classroom, his attention is most frequently directed to this area as he thinks about the experiences of his own children. You may have a similar lens. Although you cannot eliminate it, you can increase your awareness of the way it can interfere with data collection. And ultimately, you're filling the role of observer not for yourself but to collect data for the lead teacher. That teacher has requested the collection of specific data—from the wait time she provides following a question, to the student dialogue in a cooperative group—and it's your role to fulfill that request.

Making Meaning Rather Than Collecting Data

As you collect classroom data during an observation, it can be tempting to begin constructing meaning from what you are observing. You may even begin to answer the lead teacher's focus question as you review lines (and potentially pages!) of data you have gathered in his classroom. We therefore encourage you to remain focused solely on the task of data collection and not to begin interpreting or drawing conclusions about the data you have collected. There will be an opportunity to do just that, but not until the postobservation debriefing. At that point, you and your colleagues will come together—both the lead teacher and observers—to share the data, thereby widening the pool of data. This best equips the team to truly see the data and collaboratively make meaning from what has been observed.

Due to the flurry of activity inherent in a classroom environment, where dozens of minds are at work, it can be easy as the observer to try to make sense of what you're seeing as you observe. Are the students engaged? Are they thinking critically? Are the teacher's instructions clear? Is that student who has gotten out of his seat for the sixth time in ten minutes bored, anxious to get to lunch, or challenged by the assignment? The danger in making meaning of your observations while you are in the classroom is at least threefold:

- Shifting your attention to meaning making could limit your ability to collect data as thoroughly as you would be able to with your attention solely focused on collecting data.

- Meaning making is more powerful when it is done with more context and background about what has been going on in class prior to the observation and what is going to be expected from students in the coming days. Thus, the postobservation debriefing is the right opportunity to make meaning of the data because the teacher is there to provide such context.

- Presenting objective data to the teacher is the best way to ensure that the conversation remains objective and not evaluative in the postobservation debriefing. We've seen even experienced lead teachers put up defenses when they feel that the observer has violated the trust they handed to them by humbly soliciting help in the first place.

FINAL THOUGHTS

The observation experience is the opportunity to become a transparent teacher as you open the door to the collection of data that are immediately relevant to you: data on your students, your content, and your instruction. This information enables you to take charge and lead powerful conversations, renewing your team's commitment to improving instruction. Selecting data methods that best respond to your focus question will ensure that you receive relevant data and also that your observers have clarity on their roles in the classroom.

In the next chapter, we discuss what you've been waiting for: the outcome of the observation. You'll see how the data collection methods speak to the focus question. We'll discuss the structure of the postobservation debriefing meeting, and you'll watch Heather's unfold. You won't want to miss her big breakthrough.

CHAPTER FIVE
THE POSTOBSERVATION DEBRIEFING

W hew!" Heather sat down, tucking a strand of hair behind her ear. "That observation was the fastest twenty minutes of my day!" The final school bell was about to ring, and her students were zipping their notebooks into their backpacks. She overheard one big boy quip to a smaller, straight A student, "Hey, Smarty, you think you can calculate the surface area of my iPod?" The smaller boy looked up to see a lightly mocking smile and hesitated, "Um . . . "

Heather stepped in: "Well, boys, if you'd like to measure the dimensions of the iPod in question, I'm sure I can help you calculate the surface area." The bell rang, and the boys both flew out the door, grateful to avoid any more calculations.

A few minutes later, Jay and Margaret made their way in to where Heather had again arranged three chairs. They pulled out their notes from the observation and sat down for the postobservation debriefing meeting. Heather was all ears.

As a transparent teacher engaged in teacher-driven observation (TDO), you have opened your classroom door to your colleagues for a new professional development experience. It's surprising what kind of traction professional development can have when it happens right in the classroom. As students now stream out of that same doorway, you are likely curious about the next phase: What meaning will you find in the data, and how will you use these new insights to improve your instruction? One thing you do know is that observation feels good when you take charge—when you decide what you want to learn and what sort of data you want to collect. Your colleagues are equipped to help you dig into these new data, learn from the findings, and ultimately commit to instructional changes. You and your colleagues are prepared to engage in the final—and most critical—piece of teacher-driven observation: the postobservation debriefing.

PURPOSE OF THE POSTOBSERVATION DEBRIEFING

Following the observation, your observers will likely have pages of data they collected in your classroom. The postobservation debriefing is their opportunity to share these data with you, the lead teacher. Of course, sharing the data is only the first step of the postobservation debriefing. As a team, you'll explore how the data answer your focus question. How are students' leveraging one another in cooperative groups? What is the ratio of teacher-directed to student-directed instructional time?

Discussing the data is just part of the postobservation debriefing. The objective of TDO is to collect and analyze data that inform and improve teaching and learning. To that end, it's critical that the postobservation debriefing is not only an opportunity to discuss the data collected but to commit to next steps.

Key Point

The postobservation debriefing must serve as both a platform for examining the data collected as well as an opportunity to commit to how these data will inform each participant's classroom practice.

How will these data inform your future instruction? How might the observers use the data to inform their instruction? It is through a response to these questions that the practice of TDO becomes a powerful tool for professional learning. A failure to engage in the debriefing and commit to next steps lumps TDO with handfuls of other well-intentioned but shortsighted professional development methods: it may provide learning but fails to translate that learning into instructional action. Thus, it's critical that the postobservation debriefing serve as both a platform for examining the classroom data collected, as well as an opportunity to commit to how these data will inform your classroom practice.

We first discuss how you can leverage protocols to meet the three key objectives of the postobservation debriefing: use time effectively, stay focused on the evidence, and identify next steps. Then we describe the debriefing protocol so you will know how to allocate your time in this meeting. To give you a sense of how discussion might flow in the meeting, we walk you through a case study postobservation debriefing meeting with Heather, Margaret, and Jay. Studying their interaction, you find the tools you need to lead your own postobservation debriefing. Finally, we look at common missteps in this process so you can be completely prepared to engage in TDO yourself.

LEADING THE POSTOBSERVATION DEBRIEFING

As teachers, we've all engaged in collaborative dialogue with our colleagues; some of this is more productive than others. We can each recall meetings that went long past their scheduled time or those where the outlined objectives took a backseat to the direction of conversation. While these meetings are not always productive, the existing comfort and experience we have with our colleagues can lead us to think the postobservation debriefing is simply another team meeting. As you'll find in this chapter, several critical differences separate the postobservation debriefing from other collaborative experiences in which you have taken part. To start, you'll begin with an ambitious objective: to have a meaningful conversation on the data collected and identify concrete next steps within no more than a half-hour. Second, the context of the conversation—classroom data directly tied to teaching and learning—requires openness about your own teaching and your students' learning that is not regularly demanded in meetings.

To achieve the objectives of the postobservation debriefing, you'll benefit from investing the same level of preparation you put into the preobservation meeting and the observation itself. Also, you'll find that as you and your colleagues engage in the postobservation dialogue, you'll experience the return on that investment of preparation. You and your colleagues will have clarity as to how to structure the conversation to ensure you respect everyone's time and create a valuable opportunity for learning.

Key Point

To achieve the objectives of the postobservation debriefing, the lead teacher should invest the same level of preparation that he or she put into the preobservation meeting and the observation itself.

Using Protocols

A protocol—a structure for the dialogue—creates the foundation for a productive postobservation debriefing. Think of a protocol like a recipe. To bake the tantalizing cake you see pictured in the cookbook, you have to add just so many cups of flour and so much sugar. If you add more butter than the recipe calls for, your cake will not turn out. Much like a recipe specifies exactly how much of each ingredient will produce the desired results, a protocol specifies the allocation of time—keeping participants on track toward meeting their objectives. In the process of TOD, the postobservation protocol ensures you

- Use time effectively

- Stay focused on the evidence

- Identify next steps

The structure of protocols might seem foreign at first, particularly if you've worked with your colleagues for years and established patterns of communication. From our experience, collegiality, even friendship, does not ensure we meet the objectives of the meeting. Sometimes these features of our relationships can even be problematic, as we have established patterns that result in inequitable participation (we're guessing you could name instantly the most dominant voices in your faculty meetings) or

Key Point

The protocol used to guide the postobservation debriefing directly contributes to how well the lead teacher achieves the objective of TDO in relation to the focus question.

an ineffective use of time (none of us is innocent of talking about weekend plans during a Thursday afternoon department meeting). Protocols provide a structure for our conversations, promoting "habits that we wish we already had: to take the time to listen and notice, to take the time to think about what we want to say, to work without rushing, to speak less (or speak up more)."[1] The protocol you use to guide the postobservation debriefing will directly contribute to how well you achieve the objective of TDO in relation to your focus question.

A NOTE TO PRINCIPALS

You can support teachers in structuring their conversations by providing them protocols and modeling the use of protocols in the meetings you run.

Use Time Effectively   There's no doubt that time is in short supply in all schools and classrooms. From your experience juggling the immediate demands of your classroom instruction and lesson planning, along with your additional responsibilities, you can see the importance of using time as a valuable resource.

The postobservation debriefing protocol enables you to take charge of time. It guides the allocation of time for both sharing and making meaning of the data, ensuring that time remains for each critical piece of dialogue, while also keeping the momentum of the meeting toward a focus on next steps. To target the greatest lever for improvement, instruction, it's critical that you use your limited time together with your colleagues to share the data and discuss their implications for instruction.

Stay Focused on the Evidence   We view any environment, including classrooms, through the lens of our own experiences. This insight is especially important for observers. It can be difficult for classroom observers to shed the perceptions they have about particular instructional methods or, even harder, particular students. The fact that a certain student takes every ounce of your patience (Has a face popped into your head?) or that a student worked meticulously to earn an A in your class last semester can make it difficult to focus on the data objectively. You can make generalizations based on your perceptions and experiences and then easily draw conclusions about observations before you have really looked at the data carefully. When you're sharing the data you collected with the lead teacher during the postobservation debriefing meeting, you might not even be aware you've drawn a conclusion—particularly when using language (words like *bored, engaged, struggling, disruptive*) that is commonplace in educational dialogue.

The following comments illustrate what observers might say to the lead teacher when they've drawn conclusions before examining the data:

"Those students were really engaged."

"All but three of your students participated in the small group discussions. However, I had two of those students in my class last year, and they are always quiet."

"I found your lesson particularly effective because you maintained high expectations for your kids."

These comments can be problematic because they assume that lead teachers and observers share identical visions of students and classrooms described by subjective terms (from *engaged* to *effective*). Yet when you as an observer begin to describe the behaviors (instead of labeling them) you observed, you may realize that you have differing perceptions of what an engaged student looks like. Is a student who follows directions engaged? What about students in a classroom where the flurry of student conversation drowns out all other noise?

Transparent teachers maintain a focus on the evidence. By providing descriptions of what you see and hear in a classroom, you are better equipped to contribute to robust conversations about classroom data. For example, instead of writing, "Those students were really engaged," an observer could track student eye movements or script student-to-student conversations. When you start with the data, your conversations move into meaningful questions that the data elicit. What does engagement look like in the classroom? What does effective student group work look and sound like? What evidence of student understanding was observed at the end of the lesson? These questions lend themselves to collaborative inquiry and are at the heart of the practice of TDO.

Identify Next Steps   The postobservation protocol provides a structure to ensure that you, as the lead teacher, don't neglect the instructional implications of the data or your reflections on them. Without a protocol, it's common for talking—by the leader or a select few participants—to consume the meeting. Your own voice may be one of these consistently heard in meetings, or perhaps you can relate to being the individual who defers to these dominant voices. Although conversation is certainly essential to making meaning of the data collected and to informing instructional decision making, it can derail collaboration if it isn't guided by protocol.

How often have you been in a grade- or department-level meeting that never got past its first agenda item as rounds of conversation on one topic continued for thirty or forty minutes? If this problematic pattern inhabits the postobservation debriefing meeting, it will undermine the final piece: identifying the instructional implications of the data. And if you fail to reach this point in the dialogue, never identifying the next steps, then the data collected are nothing more than a superficial resource for instructional improvements. The protocol enables you to take charge of the meeting and create the results you signed up for.

THE POSTOBSERVATION DEBRIEFING PROTOCOL

The protocol we present to guide the postobservation debriefing has three distinct pieces: an opportunity for the observers to share the data, the lead teacher's reflection on the data shared, and a dialogue among the lead teacher and observers to discuss the implications of the data on instruction (figures 5.1 and 5.2). Although we present just one option for what this postobservation debriefing could look like, we believe these three pieces, focused on the data and relevant instructional responses, are critical to effective debriefing.

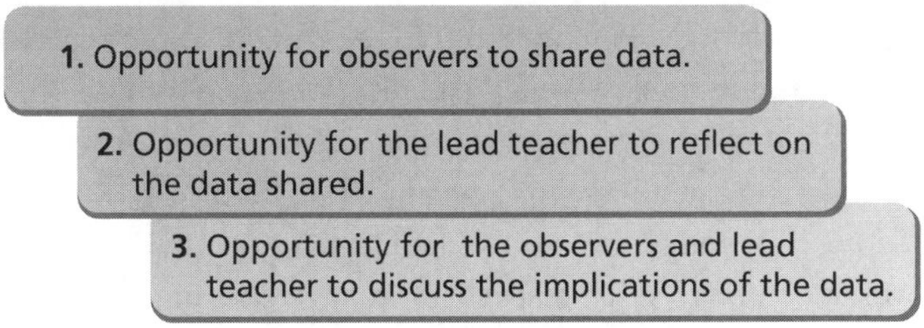

1. Opportunity for observers to share data.

2. Opportunity for the lead teacher to reflect on the data shared.

3. Opportunity for the observers and lead teacher to discuss the implications of the data.

FIGURE 5.1. Components of the Postobservation Meeting

FIGURE 5.2. Postobservation Debriefing Protocol

1. Observers discuss the teaching and learning observed.

   - In descriptive statements: What did you see and hear? (4 minutes)

   - What do you wonder about or make of this information? (4 minutes)

2. The observed teacher speaks about how the data from the observation relate to the focus question. (2 minutes)

   - How do the data answer my focus question?

   - Have the data informed other areas of my instruction and if so, how?

3. The observers and observed teacher discuss the next steps. (5 minutes)

   Observed Teacher's Questions

   - How will the data collected inform my instruction in the future?

   - Are there additional strategies I would like to try?

   - Are there areas where I want to learn more?

   Observers' Question

   - What have I learned from this experience that I can apply to my own instruction?

At times it's easy to focus on the steps of the protocol to the neglect of the time allotments. It's natural to think, "We'll just talk about each topic as long or as little as we need to." We'd caution you against entering the postobservation debriefing with this mind-set. You can guess why ignoring time limits can be problematic: it's likely the meeting will end before you've had time to identify and commit to next steps. However, it can be equally destructive to neglect using the full time allotted for each step of the protocol by preventing the deeper thinking that occurs when participants have a moment to sit with the data. You may have moments of silence during the protocol, and that's completely acceptable. As the observed teacher, you may struggle to fill a full two minutes of time with your reflections on the data. If so, wait until the full time is up before moving on, because this wait time may be just what each participant (including you) needs to have an aha! moment characteristic of TDO. We often provide wait time for our students to support their mental processing; this time during the postobservation debriefing serves an identical purpose.

Observers Discuss the Data Collected   The first phase of the protocol allocates time specifically for observers to share the data they collected. The observers are the only speakers during this first phase of the postobservation debriefing. While it can be tempting for you as the lead teacher to engage in conversation, doing so can be counterproductive to the process and to your learning. You might want to clarify certain observations, explaining your own conclusion about the data collected. If an observer shares that you called on seven of twenty-eight students in the class, you may want to explain your decision to do so. If an observer states that one student did not participate in group work, you may insist on sharing background information about the student in order to put the behavior in context. But inserting these comments undermines the objective of this first part of the protocol, which is to share data.

If you and your team are truly going to make sense of the data, particularly as they relate to your instruction, you must see all of the data before you try and construct meaning from them. Doing otherwise would be like drawing a conclusion from a science experiment without examining the data collected from the experiment itself. It would prove superficial at best. The first phase of the postobservation debriefing is explicitly chunked into two sections to create an opportunity for observers to share the data in descriptive statements and give them an opportunity to make meaning of the data. The meaning the observers construct can be posed as statements or questions. The following example illustrates this first phase of the postobservation debriefing in action as Heather and her colleagues gather following the observation of her seventh-grade math class.

Heather opens the meeting: "Margaret, why don't you start us off by sharing the questions that you scripted?"

"All right," Margaret begins. "You asked me to script and count your questions as you worked to release responsibility to students as part of the gradual release method. I scripted nineteen questions in the twenty minutes I observed. Here are some of the questions I recorded:

'What was your strategy?'

'What else are you missing to find the equation?'

'How do we find the area of a circle?' 'What's the next step?'

'2π. 2π what?'

'How are you going to use the circumference to find the area?'

"You know, a lot of questions prompted the students' thinking. My sense is that you were trying to scaffold for the students—"

"Margaret, sorry to cut you off, but I'm really interested in hearing all of the questions so we can examine the complete data you and Jay collected. We'll talk about what the data mean in a minute, but for now, it'll be most helpful for me if we stick to the data."

"Okay. Let's see. Here are the other questions I collected:

'Once you have height, what do you need to multiply by?'

'What does the r stand for?'

'What's the relationship between radius and diameter?'

'Is 2r the same as d?'

'What's the last step we need to do?'

'What's your formula?'

'How did you find the area?'

'Can you find circumference?'

'If we're calculating surface area, what do we have to do first?'

'Do you have a strategy?'

'What other information do we need?'

'What are we finding? Is that it?'

"Those are all of the questions I scripted."

"I scripted only students' questions," Jay begins. "I listened closely but recorded just three questions. Andrea asked, 'What should I do next?' Juan asked, 'Is the formula 2c times *h*?' and Zach asked, 'If that's the formula for surface area of a cylinder, what's the formula for volume?'"

"Interesting," Heather says. "Before we dig into the data even more, we have a few minutes for each of you to talk about what you make of these questions."

"Well, I'm wondering," Margaret notes, "about the role of questions in your class. When I look at the questions, it seems like some of them were more about prompting student thinking—particularly when you asked about next steps or prompted recall of a formula. As I said earlier, maybe these questions were meant to scaffold students' understanding. If that's the case, it makes me wonder if students are ready for you to release responsibility to them."

Jay adds, "You know, that has me thinking back to our earlier meeting. Before the observation, Heather, you said your objective was to release responsibility to students for finding the surface area of three-dimensional objects. I wonder if students are ready to take on this task independently or in small groups. Are the questions providing so much direction to students that maybe we don't realize how much their skills really have developed through your prior lessons on surface area?"

"You know, the other thing that catches my attention is the ratio of student to teacher questions," Margaret explains. "I wonder if you had asked fewer questions, Heather, whether the students would have been able to complete the task without your scaffolding. If so, what would the effect be of releasing even more responsibility to them, which might mean reducing the prompts and questions you provide?"

While you, like Heather, will remain quiet during this first phase of the post-observation debriefing, you simultaneously have a critical role: to collect all of the data and begin thinking about their implications for your focus question. Your observers will bring unique insights and perspectives to this process as they begin making meaning of the data.

Observed Teacher Reflects on the Data Collected In just the first eight minutes of the postobservation debriefing meeting, you've likely accomplished quite a bit. Ideas may already be swirling in your mind about how the data can inform your instruction and you may be chomping at the bit to share your thinking. Or the sheer quantity of data may require a degree of processing that seems rushed in such an efficient meeting. Either way, it's now your opportunity to explore how the data answer your focus question. You'll be thinking out loud as you process the implications of the data on your instruction.

Let's revisit Heather's postobservation debriefing to hear her reflection in action:

"You know, it's surprising to hear how many questions I asked. I've always thought questions are an effective way to prompt student thinking, but I wonder if my own questions are doing the thinking in the class. Margaret, when you shared the questions you scripted, I noticed that several of them prompted students on the next step the problem required. And now that I see the questions on paper, I'm wondering if those questions are actually preventing what I had hoped, which is that students are developing the skills to solve these problems independently. How will they do that if I'm prompting their thinking?

"Also, I'm really interested in the number of questions students asked. Only three? I didn't expect that. Based on the work I collected from students at the end of class, I think that many of them understand the process of calculating surface area. Combined with the few questions they posed to me, their work leads me to think that I need to focus less on scaffolding their thinking and more on getting them to do the thinking I've been doing for them. I think they'd benefit from an opportunity to identify the sequence of steps involved in these math problems without my direct and consistent prompting."

Teachers understand the strong relationship between teaching and learning: one cannot be meaningfully examined outside the context of the other. This phase of the postobservation debrief presents you, the lead teacher, the context to explore the relationship between teaching and student learning in your classroom as documented through the data your observers collected. Examining teaching and learning together will enhance your learning and your capacity for instructional improvement.

Observers and Observed Teacher Discuss the Next Steps You and your colleagues have now arrived at the culmination of learning within the practice of TDO: the opportunity to commit to specific instructional refinements. While your own area for development and focus question drove the process, there's a good chance your observers have been thinking about their own instruction as well. Your willingness to open your classroom door and share your instructional practice provides a context not just for your own learning but for your observers' learning

Key Point

The culmination of learning within TDO occurs during the postobservation meeting when the lead teacher and observing teachers take the opportunity to commit to specific instructional refinements.

too. Again, we return to Heather's postobservation debrief to see how she develops her next steps:

"Okay. Now we're ready to discuss next steps," Heather says. "I'll start, but feel free to jump in if you have thoughts. As I mentioned, the data you collected have really gotten me thinking about the way I use questions in my class and also about students' own abilities to monitor their thinking—particularly on problems that have several steps, like those they tackled in class today. As a teacher, I really want them to be able to identify each step in the sequence of the problem without my prompting. If they can't do that, then they really haven't developed the skill, right? This brings me back to my original focus, which was on the use of gradual release. My next step is to truly give them an opportunity to collaboratively solve these problems. I thought I was doing that, but now I realize I was still guiding the instruction.

"Next lesson, we are going to apply their skills to several other three-dimensional shapes, and I am going to provide them with an opportunity to apply their skills in small groups. Also, I'd like to learn more about getting students to think about their own thinking, to be more metacognitive. Instead of prompting their thinking, I'd like to hear their ability to think about their own thinking—to approach the math problem as a whole and identify each step necessary to solve it."

Jay adds, "You know, Heather, since I don't teach math, I wasn't sure I'd learn much from this observation, but the whole process has me thinking a lot about gradual release as well, which I use in my social studies class. I'm working on being deliberate about each stage of gradual release, and seeing you provide guided instruction to your students makes me think about how I do—or don't do—that in my own classroom. I want to be more intentional about each stage of gradual release. My kids are starting their essays next week, and I am going to use this model to help each of them develop a thesis and outline for their papers. All too often, I do it and then hand the task over to students individually. Today I realized I'm neglecting the 'we do' phase of gradual release."

"It's interesting that we are each seeing this experience through a slightly different lens," Margaret reflects. "I've been thinking about Heather's questions in her class and how I often fill the role of the questioner in my class. I wonder how I can get students to ask themselves these questions—to prompt their own thinking rather than relying on my role. Next week, as we apply linear equations to real-world problems in my math class, I am going to create an opportunity for students to brainstorm and share the questions they need to ask themselves as they begin working through a multistep problem."

"Great idea, Margaret," Heather responds. "That really hits on my hope to develop students' metacognition. I'm going to use that idea as well. Perhaps we could even touch base before and after the lesson to share our strategies and successes."

The greater the level of detail in a plan of action, the greater chance the plan has of being carried out. Imagine the likely success of two people who plan to eat more nutritious lunches at work instead of ordering out each day. Both identify the need to bring lunch, but one schedules time each Sunday afternoon to buy healthy lunch options for the week and prepare the meals. The other does no such preparation beforehand. Who's more likely to have implemented the change a week later?

Key Point

The instructional value you draw from the TDO experience will increase when you not only identify instructional changes, but commit to an occasion for these changes.

The instructional value you draw from the TDO experience will increase when you not only identify instructional changes, but commit to an occasion for these changes. Will you implement them next class? Next week? Such a commitment can ensure that despite a busy schedule, you make the improvements to instruction.

Planning a follow-up meeting with your colleagues can also provide benefit in soft accountability for implementation of the changes and revisiting the successes and struggles of implementation. Instruction is much more complex than simply implementing an idea and experiencing 100 percent success. If teaching were that simple, most of us would find it significantly less satisfying. Creating a plan to revisit the instructional focus of your observation with your colleagues can provide a valuable opportunity to explore implementation further. You, as the lead teacher, can propose this opportunity at the end of the postobservation debrief, asking your colleagues, "Would you be willing to come back to my classroom a month from now?"

And finally, as you and your colleagues wrap up the meeting, they will hand you the data they collected. This final step has both tangible and symbolic value in the process of TDO. Not only does it provide you with all of the data collected (which might have been too voluminous to note during the meeting), but it also emphasizes a critical point: that they performed the observation and collected the data to help you meet your stated goal.

Making Meaning of the Data

In this case study, Heather, Jay, and Margaret baked a picture-perfect metaphorical cake. They followed protocol by allocating specific amounts of time to specific ingredients of their debrief meeting, and they came out with meaningful next steps.

Because sequencing affects results, it's important to note that they followed the scheduled order—from examining the data at a descriptive level, to making meaning of the data, to discussing the implications for the classroom. If we fail to make meaning of the data collected, we'll never identify instructional improvements, and neither teaching nor student learning will improve.

At this point, we'd like to discuss the sequence that works best for making meaning of the data. In earlier chapters, we stressed the importance of staying descriptive during the data collection and the early portion of the postobservation debrief. However, it's equally important to make meaning and draw conclusions about the data as part of the postobservation debriefing. This is a process of intentionally climbing the ladder of inference—going from looking at the pool of data available, adding meaning, drawing conclusions, and taking actions based on these conclusions.[2] These steps are critical, but only after you've taken the time to fully examine the data collected.

As the leader of teacher-driven observation, you will likely also take the lead when, as a team, you are ready to climb the ladder. In Heather's observation, Margaret began to make meaning early. Heather provided a brief reminder to first share the data. When the data had been shared, the team then began to construct meaning, a necessary transition within the postobservation debriefing.

COMMON MISSTEPS

The postobservation debrief is the occasion when the data collected become the source of relevant learning and instructional improvements. There's no doubt that this TDO step can make or break the process. The missteps we identify impede not only the postobservation debriefing itself; they also reduce the likelihood that the practice of TDO will create meaningful learning for you. We encourage you to reread these missteps again immediately prior to leading your first postobservation debriefing in order to anticipate the ways you can avoid these barriers to a successful experience.

Staying in the "Land of Nice"

Collaborative conversations on teaching and learning often occur in the "land of nice," where conversations never analyze instructional practice.[3] This culture "inhibits the team from reaching a level of rigorous collaborative discourse where teachers are challenging each other's and their own thinking, beliefs, assumptions, and practice."[4] We hear evidence of the land of nice consistently in our work with teachers: colleagues provide affirmations of effectiveness but struggle to address improvements to teaching and learning. *You did such a great job engaging your students. You do really well with such a challenging group of kids. I learned so much from your classroom.* While these patterns are comfortable, the reason they exist in the first place, they prevent us from gaining value from our collaborative endeavors.

One way to steer clear of the land of nice is to remember that the conversations within TDO are about teaching and not a teacher, about practice and not people.[5] As the lead teacher, you play a critical role in guiding conversation and setting the tone for the conversation. You can successfully redirect the conversation by saying, "Thanks for your positive comments. I'm looking to improve my practice so I want to ensure we also talk about your observations, thoughts, and wonderings about how I can improve my instruction." And just as we model skills for our students, you can model the level of inquiry you desire from your colleagues. Don't be afraid to throw your own questions into the mix to demonstrate that you are willing and eager to examine your practice deeply.

Climbing the Ladder of Inference Too Quickly or Not Climbing It at All

It's easy to complete an observation with a singular conclusion in mind about the quality of the teaching—especially since many of the observation processes that teachers experience have led to that shortchanged result. The postobservation debriefing requires you and your observers to share and examine the data—objective observations on teaching and learning—before drawing conclusions. The protocol is designed to do just that: to provide an opportunity for you to share and examine data before making meaning. This protocol ensures that you truly see all the data before making sense of them. While we caution against climbing the ladder of inference too quickly, it's equally problematic not to climb the ladder at all. If you and your team only share the data and never discuss their meaning or draw conclusions about the implications for instruction, you fail to leverage true learning that will have an important impact on your classroom instruction and your students.

Discussion Without Commitments to Action

Dialogue is at the heart of the TDO process. Yet dialogue on teaching and learning will not in and of itself improve instruction. That can happen only through the instructional changes you make. Identifying and committing to specific instructional changes at the end of the postobservation debrief is a step toward that end. When you neglect this final step of the process, the impact of the discussion goes no further than the meeting itself.

Failure to Discuss the Relationship Between Teaching and Learning

The embedded culture within schools might lead you to feel more comfortable discussing students (and their learning) than the relationship between your teaching and student learning. The latter requires a level of transparency and vulnerability you may not be used to in your professional development. This factor often becomes an obstacle in the postobservation debriefing if you engage in conversation on student learning without ever delving into your own practice. The result? If you never discuss the relationship between teaching and learning, you'll never identify instructional improvements that can facilitate student achievement. It is only through examining the relationship between your teaching and your students' learning that you are able to become a better teacher. TDO empowers you to take charge of this examination by situating your professional development right in your own classroom.

FINAL THOUGHTS

You now have a solid understanding of how to take charge and lead your postobservation debriefing to generate solid results. You are becoming an expert at using protocols to guide efficient, focused conversation, and you know the importance of making meaning from the data your team has collected. Although the steps of teacher-driven observation are now complete, the learning process remains in full swing. The data your observers collected and shared with you have equipped you to identify instructional changes and create a plan for their implementation. You're heading back into your classroom with a greater understanding of your students, their learning, and how your instruction can better support their achievement.

In the next chapter, we discuss logistics, including the various entry points for introducing TDO to your school and your classroom. This can be a pretty gutsy thing to do, but it will make all the difference in your professional development. We'll help you think through managing key resources like time, personnel, and funding so you'll be prepared to take charge.

PART THREE

Sustaining

CHAPTER SIX
FIGURING OUT THE LOGISTICS

Afar their first experience with teacher-driven observation (TDO), Jay, Margaret, and Heather performed two more observation rounds that year. They traded roles so that each person had a chance to be the lead teacher. By coordinating their schedules carefully and being willing to commit fifteen minutes before or after school as needed, they didn't have to take much time away from their own classrooms for the meetings and observation time. Their administrators were enthusiastic about their efforts, and they helped arrange class coverage when necessary. Jay, Margaret, and Heather each noted that TDO had a long-term impact on their teaching. Heather revised her questioning strategy in releasing responsibility to her students and noticed that the transition was smoother than she expected. TDO provided a way for all three to open up their classrooms, become transparent teachers, and in doing so take charge of their professional learning.

After reading chapters 3, 4, and 5, you have a clear picture of what TDO can offer you, your students, and your school, and we're betting that you find the possibilities both compelling and exciting. We're also betting that at this point, you're taking a deep breath, wondering exactly how to pull it off. In fact, TDO can be easily managed with solid preparation. How well you plan for the logistics affects how smooth your experience with TDO is.

We are here to tell you that you're already on your way to becoming a transparent teacher: getting the vision is the first phase of the process. It takes at least one teacher with vision, motivation, and tenacity to make it happen. As you move from vision to reality, you've probably come up with a number of questions about the specifics of implementation. You're in exactly the right place. We designed this chapter to support you in taking charge of your vision of TDO in your school.

Here we illustrate how implementation might look in a variety of settings. These examples demonstrate how TDO can be effective even in environments with limited resources. We predict you'll see how TDO can serve your own learning in your own environment, even with the unique obstacles or constraints it may present. To help you figure out how to dive in, we discuss in this chapter three potential entry point models: individual, team, and schoolwide. As you read, you'll have a sense for which model might fit your needs best. We also offer details about effectively allocating three key resources: time, personnel, and funding.

PLANNING FOR IMPLEMENTATION

When you're planning a trip and arranging in advance your transportation, lodging, and activities, you can sit back and enjoy the trip as it unfolds. Careful planning leaves room for spontaneously eating at an outdoor café instead of a fancy restaurant, but it also provides structure that will support you. Equally, preparing in advance the relevant details prior to your observation process will afford you the luxury of focusing on your own learning rather than on the logistics of implementation itself. As we illustrate examples of teachers and schools engaged in this work, we also highlight ways you can leverage existing resources so you can spend your planning energy on the important parts of the observation process.

Entry Points

This section details how implementation might look with a variety of different entry points. By *entry point* we mean the initiator of the process, which could be an individual teacher, a group of teachers, or an entire faculty. Each of these entry points is just that: a place to begin TDO implementation. Each approach offers its own unique benefits. We've seen schools begin with a handful of teacher volunteers who engage in the work in small, informal networks, allowing the energy and enthusiasm from these pockets of work to take hold in larger groups. Excitement and momentum then grow organically through the building as teachers engaging in teacher-driven observation have positive experiences with the process and the learning they have cultivated from their engagement in it. Some schools take an opposite approach, first engaging all faculty members in the TDO process in an attempt to get the work started more quickly. Their first round of observations is framed as a learning round—an opportunity to learn the structure of the process. With a common schoolwide understanding of TDO in place, the school then moves from a schoolwide model to a flexible model, in which teachers identify their own networks and voluntarily participate in the process. In one instance, we saw one school's successes lead several other schools in their geographic feeder pattern to implement similar observation processes.

Throughout the preceding chapters, we've explored the TDO process through the lens of the lead teacher. Although the lead teacher is at the heart of the process, from identifying a focus all the way through the personal learning articulated in the postobservation debriefing, the process can have an impact on the work of an entire team, school, or even district.

Key Point

While the lead teacher is at the heart of teacher-driven observation, this process can have an impact on the work of an entire team, school, or even district.

As you read the upcoming sections, look for which entry point will make the most sense for your own school context and your particular role.

Individual Model   At its most organic level, TDO begins as an individual's quest for more substantial professional learning and growth. We purposely use the word *organic* here to mean "without the help of outside stimulants." We have noticed that some, if not all, of the stickiest ideas in education have started with individual teachers who have a vision and try it out on their own. Then, organically, the practices grow into system standards.

Consider a teacher who wants to improve her practice and craves professional collaboration grounded in the realities of her classroom, her instruction, and her students, so she elicits the help of colleagues who may or may not be familiar with TDO. Heather, the middle school math teacher featured in previous chapters, illustrates this individual approach.

Key Point

The individual model puts the greatest amount of responsibility on the lead teacher and provides the greatest autonomy for that teacher.

This individual entry point, where a single teacher engages others in one observation, most closely aligns with the spirit of TDO as a teacher-led professional learning opportunity. The timing of and learning from the observation are authentically grounded in the lead teacher's own interest. While this model puts the greatest amount of responsibility on the lead teacher, it simultaneously provides the greatest level of autonomy for the teacher. She alone chooses what the focus will be and who will enter her classroom. And because she alone has identified each of the details, there is clarity in whom the observation serves: the lead teacher.

You can imagine a teacher identifying an on-the-spot need on a Monday and inviting peers into her classroom later that week to collect data and problem-solve. With only one classroom observation, the logistics are relatively straightforward, particularly if the teachers have common planning time built into their schedule. As illustrated through Heather's experience, TDO created little scheduling disruption and, due in part to the support of her colleagues, required only the resource of time. It simultaneously required a level of understanding of and comfort with the TDO process. Heather's capacity to identify a specific focus and lead a small team of peers through the process was fundamental to its success.

Thus, the individual model requires a level of capacity that other models do not. From a conceptual understanding of the TDO process to group facilitation skills to the attention to detail required to plan for the pre- and postobservation conversations, the individual model flourishes when lead teachers bring these skills to the table. And while the individual model may best respond to a teacher's learning needs, it can lack the cohesive nature and collaborative focus other models offer, as the following sections illustrate.

One of the secrets of the individual model is its potential to grow organically. We were once working with a leadership team from a school labeled as "needs improvement" by its state. The leadership team's role was to identify and implement school improvement initiatives. We introduced TDO to the team. Well versed in returning from such sessions, prepared to recount team decisions to their staff, the team made a plan to introduce TDO to their faculty, along with an implementation plan for the whole school. The team was rightfully concerned about the faculty's reaction to yet another initiative, so we recommended that in lieu of announcing a new initiative to the school, each team member simply invite a few peers to help him or her improve in a focus area. No announcement was made. The team didn't even name the model; each member humbly asked a few peers to come and observe.

The result was that after one year, nearly every teacher at the school had participated in a round of observations, and over half the faculty had invited at least one group to their own classrooms. Several teachers commented on an end-of-year survey that the observations were the most powerful professional development activity of their entire careers, despite serious spending from the district and state on more formal initiatives. The leadership team was convinced that the value of TDO would have been nowhere near what it achieved if they had gone back to the school and "announced" the plan.

Team Model   Small teams of teachers can also be an effective entry point for TDO. The teams can be within departments or grade levels, or just groups of teachers who eat lunch together. They can choose to do a round of observations together, where each teacher is both a lead teacher (identifying the focus for his observation) and an observer in the classrooms of colleagues. This round of observations can occur in one day or over several days.

Key Point

Teacher-driven observation can leverage and build on existing teams, adding a meaningful component that more closely links collaborative opportunities to instructional improvements.

More often than not, we've seen existing teams (professional learning communities, communities of practice, grade levels, a group of new teachers) decide together to take this on because they may already share common planning time that they can leverage for pre- or postobservation conversations. Teacher-driven observation can leverage and build on these collaborative structures, adding a meaningful component that more closely links collaborative opportunities to instructional improvements. Imagine how much more robust conversations in professional learning communities become when participants talk about student work data and classroom observation data. The conversations can shift from ideas on how to address student learning needs to the implementation of those ideas.

Less formal school networks may also serve as a team structure for TDO. For example, in one high school, a group of cross-content-area teachers came together informally to engage in a book study, the topic of which served as the foundation for participants' focus questions and observations. These groups may be even more organic: two teachers, using their hall duty time to discuss their challenges with classroom management with student work groups, decide to engage in a round of TDO together.

Whether the teams already exist or are formed from common interests, you may find value in engaging in TDO with others who share students, content, or an interest in a particular area of instructional improvement. With a shared focus—whether it be increasing student engagement or refining the implementation of Socratic seminar—you can use the collective expertise, experience, and classroom data to analyze your focus questions.

Besides serving as a natural entry point for TDO, teams also provide a convenient context for an ongoing TDO process, one in which teachers can revisit a student need or strategy over the course of time or each team member can lead the process a few times throughout a school year. Teachers often cite the value of a consistent TDO team because they can study a topic and its implications for instruction over the course of several months or an entire school year.

Schoolwide Model   The schoolwide TDO model is an extension of the team model, as it involves several teacher teams engaged in TDO across an entire school and implies schoolwide participation over a period of weeks or months. A schoolwide model can serve as a starting point for TDO, providing an opportunity for all teachers to learn and develop comfort with the process. An administrator or group of teacher leaders may choose the entire school as the entry point when fast implementation is in order.

Schoolwide engagement in TDO can facilitate a broad culture of collaboration, particularly among teachers who may not otherwise have opportunities to work together. Schoolwide models may leverage existing team structures in a building or promote cross-department and cross-grade collaboration through new teams. Imagine the diversity of perspectives and expertise of a high school teacher team comprising teachers of chorus, chemistry, health, and English!

Key Point

The schoolwide model for engaging in TDO can facilitate a broad culture of collaboration, particularly among teachers who may not otherwise have opportunities to work together.

When all teachers in a building engage in TDO, there is collective momentum toward building comfort in opening classroom doors, breaking down the professional isolation common in many schools, and becoming transparent teachers. This level of shared and open practice becomes the way of doing business among a faculty that engages in schoolwide TDO. Conversations about instruction become a common feature of professional dialogue.

Schools that implement a schoolwide round of observations find that one of its greatest advantages exists in its ability to demystify the process. Let's be honest: one of the biggest barriers to TDO is the anxiety about opening up our practice to

A NOTE TO PRINCIPALS

This schoolwide entry point in particular relies heavily on your support. The next chapter will help you understand more thoroughly how you can help support your teachers who are seeking involvement of the whole school.

peers. The most frequent questions we hear are predictable because of the isolated nature of the teaching profession: Will the process truly be nonevaluative? Will I find the process meaningful? What if a student derails my lesson plan? Seasoned TDO participants consistently cite their first experience with the process as the point at which their anxiety was replaced by excitement and value for the process. Creating an opportunity for all teachers to engage in TDO lays the groundwork for ongoing schoolwide participation.

Of course, engaging all faculty members in a round of TDO presents its own challenges. The sheer logistics of a schedule that equips dozens or even hundreds of teachers to observe one another can be daunting. Creating a plan and allocating the resources for these observations may reduce the level of autonomy teachers have in the process, particularly in selecting when and who observes. Without careful communication, a schoolwide approach can undermine authentic engagement as teachers ask, "If this is a project that is truly teacher driven, why don't I have control over when the observation occurs or who my observers are?"

We have seen schools successfully negotiate these challenges (see chapter 8 for one example) and create a schoolwide professional learning structure that provides teachers an authentic opportunity to identify an area of interest and examine it through classroom data. As long as teachers and school leaders maintain a vision on that singular objective, each of the models discussed—individual, teacher, or schoolwide—can facilitate meaningful, relevant professional learning for teachers.

Although each of the models discussed has pros and challenges, deciding which one is best for your school requires careful consideration of the pluses and the negatives alongside other factors that are unique to your school (see table 6.1).

Key Point

The entry point that you choose depends on your school's context and the role of the individual who initiates it.

TABLE 6.1 MODELS FOR TEACHER-DRIVEN OBSERVATION

Model	Pros	Challenges
Individual model: Single teacher engages others in one observation	Timing of and learning from observation are grounded in teacher's own interest Provides the greatest amount of autonomy to lead teacher Logistics are relatively straightforward Great potential to grow organically	Puts the greatest amount of responsibility on the lead teacher Requires a greater level of capacity than other models: lead teacher must be able to identify focus and lead peers in the process on her own Can lack a cohesive nature and collaborative focus offered by other models
Team model: Small teams of teachers engage in observations	Can use existing teams or create new teams to build on existing collaborative structures Teams can choose to do rounds together (each teacher serves as both lead and observer) Provides opportunities for robust conversations among teams Teams provide context for ongoing TDO process	Logistics may be more difficult to arrange (e.g., when you will meet, who will cover classes) if preexisting teams that do not share a common planning time engage in TDO Some existing teams may not offer the same opportunities for diversity as the individual model (e.g., grade-level teams won't have observers from other grade levels)

TABLE 6.1 MODELS FOR TEACHER-DRIVEN OBSERVATION (*CONTINUED*)

Model	Pros	Challenges
Schoolwide model: Involves several teams across entire school and implies schoolwide participation	Provides an opportunity for all teachers to develop comfort with the TDO process Allows fast implementation of TDO Facilitates a broad culture of collaboration Allows cross-grade and cross-department interaction among teachers Creates a collective momentum toward building comfort schoolwide to collaboratively engage in conversations about teaching and learning	Logistics can be daunting Creating ownership among members of a large faculty

Allocating Resources

An improvement process can have real value for you as a lead teacher only if the fundamental ideas can be translated into the realities of your school. In other words, before TDO can become a process for professional learning, it must be a process that can be reasonably implemented with the resources available to you and your school. In the remainder of this chapter, we explore how the preobservation meeting, observation, and postobservation debriefing can be structured to best leverage the valuable resources available in schools. The examples provided from schools engaged in this work illustrate that a sincere desire for improved professional learning and some creative thinking can together ensure that the concept of TDO becomes a reality.

Key Point

Implement TDO in a way that is reasonable, considering the resources available to you and your school.

Time   As a teacher, you have many needs pulling for your time—from the immediate demands of classroom teaching to the planning and preparation required for effective instruction (and, of course, the many other responsibilities that pull attention from those fundamental tasks). You'll probably agree that the resource in shortest supply at schools is time, and there's no denying that TDO requires time—for the preobservation conversation, observation, and collaborative debriefing.

Schools have taken a variety of approaches to allocating time for the steps of TDO. In some buildings, teachers leverage existing time, an approach that is particularly realistic when a single teacher is observed, as the meeting objectives can be achieved in as little as fifteen minutes. The following examples illustrate these methods in action:

- *Common planning time.* A fifth-grade team uses its Wednesday common planning period to conduct the preobservation meeting for each teacher. With four team members and strict adherence to their preobservation protocol, they are each able to lead a quick round within the hour-long meeting to prepare the others for the next day's observations. They come together on Friday, again using their hour of common planning time to conduct the postobservation debriefing for each observation.

- *Before and after school.* A middle school teacher asks his observers to meet twenty minutes before the school day begins in order to frame the midday observation. He and his observers meet again as soon as the final bell rings, concluding the debriefing in just twenty minutes.

- *Lunch time.* A high school teacher invites her two observers to eat lunch in her classroom as they discuss the focus of her sixth-period observation. They finish the preobservation conversation with time to spare and spend the remainder of lunch discussing their summer plans. As the observers prepare to leave at the end of lunch, the lead teacher reminds them they'll meet back in her room at lunch tomorrow to debrief the observation.

The logistics for the observation itself can require more ingenuity, as it may demand teaching coverage for the observers (we explore this in more detail later). As the lead teacher, you may also invite peers who have a planning period during the class you have identified for the observation, as Heather does in chapter 3.

It is important to remember that the observation itself does not need to be a full teaching period. In fact, we suggest just the opposite based on our experience: usually fifteen to twenty minutes is plenty of time to capture a wealth of data to inform a response to the lead teacher's focus question. We've found that after this time, the level of new data collected declines, resulting in diminishing returns for the observers and the observed teacher. You can imagine that had Heather's observers stayed in her classroom for a full sixty minutes instead of fifteen, they likely would have had a similar data set: a wealth of teacher questions relative to students' questions. As a lead teacher, carefully identifying the classroom time that will provide the context for relevant and robust data collection will enable you to maximize data collection in an efficient observation window.

Personnel   If release time is necessary for you to engage in TDO, the resources required may involve the allocation of support personnel in your building. Again, there are numerous ways to ensure you and your observers have the flexibility to engage in this practice. Here are several ways we have seen teachers find classroom coverage for observations:

- *Administrators.* Administrators are, not surprisingly, excited about opportunities for teachers to engage in relevant, classroom-based professional learning. This excitement often translates into a willingness to support the process through available professional development funding for release time and in an offer to cover a class for an observer. These administrators volunteer to take the reins of a classroom for twenty minutes or more, providing flexibility for teachers to enter others' rooms as observers.

- *Educational support staff.* Schools generally have a cadre of educational support personnel (from instructional assistants to special education coteachers) who are equipped to provide classroom instruction or manage a classroom for the time a teacher may need to leave the room temporarily. Enlisting these others can be an efficient and cost-effective way to engage in TDO.

- *Substitute teachers.* Substitute teachers can be one of the great unleveraged daily resources in a school building. On a handful of occasions, we've seen substitutes read the newspaper during a teacher's planning period, sitting idly until the next period arrives. This is not for lack of desire to help, but simply because all too often a substitute is scheduled to cover only one teacher's classes. Particularly in buildings with block scheduling, this can result in an hour or more of time for which a substitute is in the building but is not directly engaged with students. Some schools have found creative ways to use these substitutes. For example, one maintained a list of all planned teacher absences and informed teachers of corresponding substitute availability with adequate time to prepare. This model of coverage for TDO occurred without using a dollar more or a minute more of internal personnel time.

Funding If time is the resource in greatest demand in schools, certainly funding is a close second. While not all schools have the financial resources to support release time for TDO, some schools prioritize professional development funds for this purpose, recognizing that the return on investment often yields teacher learning that surpasses more traditional training sessions.

For example, imagine the school that hires four substitutes in one day. These substitutes provide coverage for four teachers for the first half (four periods) of the day. During period 1, the teachers each conduct a preobservation meeting, followed by four observations during periods 2 and 3. By period 4, the teachers are ready to debrief the observations. Another four teachers engage in the same process for the second half of the day (four periods). At the day's end, eight teachers have engaged in professional learning that has direct application for their teaching the next day. It's hard to imagine many other professional development opportunities that can translate the cost of four substitutes into meaningful instructional improvement.

Many schools find ways to implement this practice by leveraging existing time without needing to tap into additional funding. However, if you are implementing TDO in a way that requires extra funding, this list can help you think creatively about where to find such funds:

- *Title I.* This is just the kind of instructional improvement work for which Title I funds were made. Consider choosing focus questions that focus on low-income students, for example.

- *Professional development funds.* These funds are often planned at least a year in advance, so why not get your request in now for next year?

- *School improvement plan funds.* Consider how the TDO process can support the improvement goals you've set as a school, and allocate funds accordingly.

- *Implementation funds.* If you use TDO to help implement Common Core State Standards, a new curriculum, or a new instructional framework (perhaps the one that your district is using for its teacher evaluation system), there are often implementation funds aligned with those initiatives that you can leverage.

- *Parent and community groups.* We've seen outside groups get excited about TDOs and leverage their fundraising and donation capabilities in support of the process.

COMMON MISSTEPS

Thinking through the logistics of TDO will benefit from the same level of thoughtfulness and preparation you invest in the process of TDO itself. Attention to the knowledge you have of your colleagues, your school, and the resources available will ensure you are best equipped to launch TDO—either in a small pocket or schoolwide. Taking note of the following common missteps can help set you up for success, ensuring that TDO becomes both a feasible and powerful opportunity for professional learning.

Making Too Big a Fuss with the Entry

Lead teachers: if you get bound up in how you can get your whole school to do this process, you may struggle to get it off the ground. Our advice is to roll with it. We assume most readers will be teachers who choose to do TDO on their own, hoping to create opportunities to improve themselves. If that describes you, then don't overthink this—just pick a few colleagues and invite them into your classroom. Choose your focus question, arrange your logistics, and then let the process unfold. Stick to your schedule, and enjoy the ride.

If you are a teacher with a formal leadership role or an administrator who wants to see this process across your whole school or district, we still suggest starting small. Helping a few teachers have a positive experience with TDO may be a better first step toward participation by the whole school than announcing your plan for whole school adoption through a staffwide e-mail. You know your staff best, though, so balance your knowledge of your staff with our advice, and go for it.

Summoning More Time and Money Than Available

Like any other project, it's easy to turn this project into something that drains time and money. We encourage you to be vigilant in keeping it simple. Look for the simplest solutions in answer to questions like these: "Who's available during this time frame to observe my class?" "I have so much going on in my class. How can I step out to observe and meet with my peers?" As we discussed in this chapter, the answer may be as uncomplicated as sitting together during lunch, taking fifteen minutes from your planning period, or asking an already on-campus substitute to cover your class during his preparation period.

Leaping Before You Look

Just as it's easy to get mired in logistics, it's also tempting to leap before you've laid the basic groundwork for your success. You can start this observation process quickly; just make sure you've thought through the necessary details we've described in this chapter so you (and everyone else who is involved) can enjoy the journey. And remember to choose a focus question that sincerely matters to you and that you can answer only through observers' data collection. Investing a bit of time in preparation will really pay off.

FINAL THOUGHTS

We hope we have made it clear that TDO requires some logistical planning, whether your entry point is as an individual teacher or a team. And if you are ambitious enough to begin the process with your entire school, then the logistics might even feel overwhelming. That said, some careful planning and a little bit of creative thinking can go a long way in ensuring that you have the resources you need to become a transparent teacher and place your professional learning squarely in the environment in which you work every day. When you become a transparent teacher, you find strategies and techniques that work for your students in your classroom. Student learning increases, as does your satisfaction in being a teacher, and your efforts to handle logistics are well worth the investment.

The next chapter is written specifically for principals and administrators. Throughout this book, we've addressed you—lead teachers—because you will be leading and participating in this work. As we talk to principals in chapter 7, we describe how they can support you in taking charge of your professional development. We discuss what roles they'll need to fill in terms of implementation in the entire school and in building internal capacity to sustain the process over the long term. We particularly encourage you to read this chapter if you are working with a whole-school entry point for TDO. If you are working with an individual entry point and you would like to involve your whole school in TDO, consider sharing this chapter (and this entire book) with your principal to help him or her catch the vision.

CHAPTER SEVEN

FOR PRINCIPALS: HOW TO IMPLEMENT AND SUSTAIN TEACHER-DRIVEN OBSERVATION

We wanted a chapter that focuses on principals because every principal we've met over the years has expressed the desire to make a long-term difference in his or her school. In the same breath, many principals express frustration that the initiatives and strategies they are implementing to make that difference don't actually deliver long-term benefits. You might be in the same boat: working to make solid gains in student learning and teacher development, but struggling to find a method that generates sustainable improvement with real-time results.

This first key point is a big claim, but we stand by it. Are you working with Common Core State Standards (CCSS) standards? Wanting to implement Marzano's new instructional framework?[1] Hoping to deliver on a thematic planning initiative? Waiting to see the value from the English language acquisition training last summer? Teacher-driven observation (TDO)

Key Point

Teacher-driven observation has the capacity to help your teachers get value out of every initiative you are implementing in your school. The process enables teachers to zoom in on aspects of the initiatives that affect their classrooms and their students.

enables your teachers to zoom in on aspects that affect their classrooms and their students and collaborate to improve implementation.

With your support, TDO can grease the wheels on your efforts to make a long-term difference—effectively helping you do better what you are already trying to do. It is a solid process your teachers can rely on to strengthen their teaching and thereby improve student learning. In this chapter, we'll walk you through what you need to know to support teachers in implementing and sustaining the practice.

IMPLEMENTING TEACHER-DRIVEN OBSERVATION

So, what exactly is your role as principal? As you can tell from the name *teacher-driven observation*, teachers lead this process. It enables them to take charge of what they want to improve in their teaching and provides them the means for embedding that professional learning right in their classrooms. Through the rest of this chapter, we provide guiding statements for your benefit. We'll point out where you can help teachers and model elements of the work for them. As you read through the other chapters in this book, you'll see ideas that you can apply to your own school. Some of your capacity to help teachers will come from your vantage point at the head of the school, but most of it will arise from your style as an educator and motivator.

For instance, the first thing we encourage you to do is to cultivate a learner disposition among teachers in your school. How you do this will depend on the teachers you're working with, what skills they already have, and what you're specifically good at providing them. Some principals model this skill; some choose staff members to model skills during faculty meetings. Some principals prefer to leave teachers more autonomy in their process and stick with the role of motivator. You know best what resources you have to work with and who your teachers are. We are confident that you can develop appropriate specifics to support them through this TDO process.

Cultivate a Learner Disposition

To embed TDO into the process of professional learning in your school, you first need to cultivate within your teams the skills that make it effective. Most important, helping teachers embrace a learner disposition is paramount to implementing the TDO process successfully.

A learner disposition—attention and focus on learning for improvement—is at the very heart of TDO. Simply put, teachers who have a learner disposition are more likely to engage in meaningful learning and personal improvement than those who don't. In fact, a teacher who is open to learning and has an orientation toward continuous improvement is on the path to an effective experience even before it begins.

You'll recognize certain behaviors in teachers who already have a strong disposition for learning: they are the first to volunteer to engage in TDO. In

Key Point

Helping teachers embrace a learner disposition is paramount to successfully implementing the TDO process. Your role as principal positions you to cultivate this disposition yourself and in your colleagues.

fact, they are often already engaging in less formal opportunities to learn from classroom observation data such as videotaping themselves teaching. For example, some teachers encourage parents to come in and observe. Others actively seek administrator observations beyond those required by the district. Some teachers collaborate with colleagues to learn a new technique or observe how they manage difficult behavioral situations. While the purposes for and structure of these observations differ fundamentally from what we're describing in this book, they confirm that observation is a useful tool for gathering data and learning the trade.

As you consider the teachers in your school who employ observation as a means to improve their practice, you'll see that they value transparency and embody the learner disposition we are discussing here. If you don't have teachers in your school who already exhibit these behaviors, watch for a notable transition as you embed TDO into the professional development culture within your school.

Some teachers who are ripe for the TDO process may never have openly invited others into their classrooms. Their learner disposition may be overshadowed by their anxiety about opening up their classroom doors. In other words, they are excited about learning and self-improvement but are more comfortable doing so from a book or at a conference. For others, an unproductive experience with prior observations—or, worse, a visitor who was judgmental, critical, superficial, or mean-spirited—has cast a shadow on the power of observation. We've found that teachers' prior experiences with classroom visitors directly correlate with their anxiety levels about inviting others into their classrooms. High anxiety can dim or even hide an otherwise strong disposition for learning.

This is where you come in: your role as principal positions you to cultivate a learner disposition in yourself and your colleagues. As you model the work, link TDO with professional development, use data, and leverage collaboration, teachers will learn these essential skills. They'll gain confidence with the observation process, and anxiety will recede as excitement builds.

Key Point

How you choose to begin implementing the TDO process will depend on the experiences that teachers at your school bring to the table.

Model the Work

There are many ways to begin TDO that are relevant from your vantage point. Our favorite kickoff strategy involves showing how TDO can make a difference for teachers. As the principal, you are uniquely situated to model a round of observation using faculty meeting time for a team to conduct a pre- or postobservation meeting, or both. We have found that creating a fishbowl environment can be effective: the participating team sits in a small circle within a larger circle of colleagues who watch in order to learn the process. Your efforts to illuminate the process can jump-start a dormant learner disposition and help potential participants overcome lingering anxieties about classroom visitors.

The key to successfully modeling the process is choosing a confident and capable lead teacher—one who is able to guide the conversation skillfully according to the chosen protocol. This teacher should have the capacity to humbly correct participating teachers when they stray from data-driven statements or invite participants to share more thorough, detailed descriptions of the data they collected. Keeping the meeting focused on the task at hand and staying within the time limits are additional prerequisite skills for lead teachers in model meetings.

Just because modeling is our favorite strategy doesn't mean it will be the best for your building, though. In some schools, kicking off a schoolwide TDO process with a modeling session may backfire. While teachers who adopt TDO quickly often have many of the required skills already, some teachers need more guidance cultivating leadership skills before they can successfully begin a round of TDO. If your teachers' skills are in a more emergent state, our advice is to kick off with one of the other methods we describe. Then, once lead teachers emerge and perhaps even self-identify as having engaged in successful rounds, modeling in front of the staff will be more productive.

Link Teacher-Driven Observation with Other Professional Development Opportunities

What is your school's main initiative for this year? Are you working on one from last year as well? Many principals we've worked with focus their staff's collective energy on an area or two for improvement each year. For instance, some schools are centering their professional development efforts on implementing new standards. Others may be emphasizing the development of strategies to meet the needs of targeted student populations. Some school departments are examining how to integrate new texts into the curriculum. Each of these areas, along with myriad others, represents a space inside a school where TDO can make a difference. For instance, you can help teachers at your school who may be wondering, "Where do I begin to identify my own focus?" to consider one of these initiatives as an accessible starting point.

As you sift through what you know already about the TDO process, we invite you to look for a link between one of those elements and your school's initiative. This book empowers teachers to gather data in classroom observations that inform and improve their teaching. So consider how the implementation of your school's current initiative could benefit from the data available in classrooms. Let's look briefly at how some schools have made this connection.

In one high school, teachers engaged in several professional development days over the course of the year to learn how to embed higher-order thinking questions in their classrooms. This professional development responded to several years of assessment data that showed a lack of such skills among the high school's significant population of students from low-income families. Interested in mastering the strategies they had learned, several teachers developed focus questions related to embedding higher-order thinking questions in their instruction. Thereby, they linked their individual focus for learning with an existing area of schoolwide emphasis.

In another school, two big initiatives were looming: implementation of the CCSS and a new teacher evaluation process. Teachers at this school chose one of these two collective focus areas and created TDO groups accordingly. Teachers within the CCSS groups chose a standard on which they would focus their attention. They developed lessons that they believed would lead to mastery of those standards and used that foundation as the focus for their first TDO round. Imagine how much more prepared for CCSS implementation these teachers became by digging into the standards together for an authentic learning opportunity.

The other group of teachers connected TDO with the new teacher evaluation model. They analyzed the various criteria on which they would eventually be evaluated. Several teachers, for example, chose guided practice as a component of the new evaluation model they wanted to work on. For this analysis, they developed focus questions. One fourth-grade teacher asked: "How is my live feedback helping students as they practice the skill I'm teaching?" A sixth-grade math teacher wondered: "How can I more effectively guide students toward the right answer without taking away their ownership for their own learning?" Imagine how much more prepared these teachers felt when their turn came to be evaluated. They had already analyzed the components of the model, worked to master specific criteria, and leveraged peer observation to perfect their approach.

It's easy to see that you'll have greater success implementing TDO across your entire school if you link it with a schoolwide initiative or focus area. By making such connections, you will integrate TDO into the fabric of the school and help teachers feel comfortable with the process. If your school doesn't have lead teachers in place, this process will develop lead teachers you can potentially call on for a schoolwide modeling session.

Key Point

You will have greater success implementing TDO across your entire school if you link it with a schoolwide initiative or focus area.

Use Data

Data in the classroom can be like the snowflakes in a well-shaken snow globe: they are everywhere. From the student work piled on teachers' desks, to the classwide results on the latest end-of-unit assessment, to the student dialogues from yesterday's group work, teachers are surrounded by data. From your vantage point in the front office, you are uniquely positioned to support teachers as they sift these data into usable, relevant categories. You can guide teachers in using these data sources, among many others, as the context for identifying and developing areas for learning.

The biggest challenge you'll face in this endeavor is matching your efforts to what the teacher you're supporting specifically needs. This can be a balancing act.

On one hand, if you help her identify a need by pointing out things she can improve, she may not respond well and may not feel she can take charge. On the other hand, if a teacher has a strong disposition for learning and comes to you for assistance in determining where she should focus her observation, you have the capacity to look into the data with her and help her decide. It's more important for you to support teachers in the learning process than it is for you to point out the most glaring thing they could improve. In other words, the disposition matters more than the focus area.

Now let's look at specific places you can offer assistance with data. At the outset of the TDO process, teachers need to develop a focus question because this drives the rest of the observation. In fact, many teachers get stalled here. You can help your teachers organize and use available data as they script their focus questions in these ways:

- *Guide them to concentrate not on what they taught but on what students learned.* For example, in what content areas did students demonstrate the least proficiency on the most recent assessment? This idea provides an opportunity for teachers to dig into how they can more effectively teach specific content or specific students.

- *Help them identify a need.* To support team-based learning, you may decide to analyze grade- or department-level data to identify a student learning need that could be relevant to the teacher. Beginning with an area of need can provide the space for an orientation toward learning and improvement.

- *Encourage them to use feedback data as a starting place.* What areas were noted for improvement on her most recent round of teacher evaluations? How can you support teachers in gaining these skills through TDO? These data can lead to creating highly relevant focus questions in the early stages of TDO.

Leverage Collaboration

Certainly the learning process within TDO is a collaborative endeavor. By its very nature, it requires the assistance and perspective of a team of colleagues. These teams don't have to wait until the observation to collaborate as peers. Instead, encourage them to engage in conversations within their grade or content area to identify and discuss areas of interest and learning. We have yet to visit a school where these conversations do not already occur informally in offices and over lunch.

Not surprisingly, having a disposition toward learning can cultivate the same trait in others. As you identify areas for improvement or growth in your leadership and your school, you create an environment where others are willing to do the same. A focus on improvement then becomes the norm as teachers learn to identify areas of need. When we as leaders openly acknowledge that we don't have all the answers, teachers are more likely to do the same. The result is a school culture focused on learning and improvement.

Key Point

As you identify areas for improvement or growth in your leadership and your school, you create an environment where others are willing to do the same.

Facilitate Planning

Although the lead teacher has the responsibility for planning the pre- and post-observation meetings, he or she will benefit from your support. Not only can you model how to plan for TDO, you can also help out with coordinating schedules and arranging substitutes to cover classes during the observation or meeting times. With such a long list of items related to the observation, along with teaching itself, teachers will appreciate every ounce of support you can give them in their planning.

Effective planning for TDO is a key lever for maximizing the benefit teachers receive from their efforts. Lead teachers who neglect the details can easily become confused or downright frustrated. It would be like flying to Paris without bothering to make hotel reservations or study maps. The trip will work—you'll survive—but ironing out details in advance will certainly smooth out your time there. When you focus on both the big-picture objectives of TDO alongside the finer details of the process, you're best equipped to meet its objectives.

At times, you can support teachers in determining where and when the pre-observation meeting and postobservation debriefing will occur and in preparing materials, including the protocol and an observation template, for their observers. These details can easily be overshadowed by the day-to-day responsibilities they

Key Point

Your support is integral during the planning phase of the TDO process.

face, but both the lead teacher and the observers will benefit from attention to detail going into the TDO process.

If your experiences are anything like our own, you know that good planning goes only so far without clear communication. It's no fun to be on either end of the questions: "You expected me to be where? When?" Help teachers avoid putting their observers in that position by ensuring that they develop a plan and communicate it clearly. While the skills of planning may appear simple in comparison with others embedded in the TDO process, neglecting the details can impede the effectiveness of the process.

Model Facilitation

As the principal, you can help lead teachers succeed in their role as facilitators. They shoulder a lot of responsibility for planning and teaching during the observation, but they are equally responsible for strong facilitation. One of the most neglected skills in collaborative settings is facilitation. All too often, teachers focus on the content of the meeting because they need to come to a decision on x or discuss y, and they neglect the process for getting there.

As the facilitator of the preobservation focus meeting and postobservation debriefing, the lead teacher bears responsibility for maintaining a focus on the meeting objectives and the process that will ensure the team meets those objectives. The protocols they use (whether taken from this book or developed individually) should assist the process of the pre- and postobservation conversations. Like a paintbrush, the protocol functions only as effectively as those who use it. As facilitators, lead teachers will work to ensure their team adheres to the protocol. This may mean assigning a timekeeper (or keeping time themselves) to ensure they meet the meeting objectives in the time allotted. Particularly in the postobservation debriefing, when the team may be inclined to make meaning of the data before first sharing them, the facilitator must remind participants of the protocol and the rationale for it.

These tasks are often easier said than done. It can be particularly difficult to redirect conversations in team meetings that have established patterns of dialogue. However, when teachers enter a meeting with clear objectives and maintain a focus on their achievement, they're better equipped to meet these facilitative demands.

From your years in education, you're familiar with how, in collaborative settings, some voices are more likely to be heard than others. As the principal, you can promote equitable participation by bringing otherwise reluctant voices into the conversation or reminding dominant voices to open the space for participation. By seeing you model this skill, your lead teachers will learn it as one of the responsibilities of an effective facilitator.

The skills of facilitation are critical to leveraging the collective expertise that is available from the team in the pre- and postobservation conversations. There's a reason that each participant is in that meeting: each brings diverse experiences, expertise, and personality. It would be a shame to fail to harness the value each brings to the experience. Simple tools can ensure success. For example, you can encourage shared participation by using a "round the horn" protocol where individuals speak one after another, traveling around a circle or a group until all members have spoken.

Teachers become more effective facilitators by engaging in the role of facilitator. They'll develop greater comfort in the challenges the role presents, from redirecting the conversation or encouraging equitable participation, as they gain facilitation experience. You can create opportunities for them to develop this experience.

Adopting the role of facilitator requires a shift in thinking. You can help teachers become aware of the differences between leading grade- or department-level meetings and facilitating TDO meetings by setting the expectation that facilitation matters in all settings, including those outside TDO.

Key Point

In TDO, simple facilitation tools help position the lead teacher for success.

When all meetings at your school have a designated facilitator, the entire faculty develops these skills and focuses on achieving diverse meeting objectives. When you cultivate your teachers' facilitation skills using TDO, you'll find benefit in all collaborative work. Watch for changes in how your teachers collaborate during department meetings and in professional learning communities. You'll notice the difference in the way they lead parent meetings and meetings for individualized education programs as well. Building facilitative capacity is an investment well worth making.

Engage in Improvement-Oriented Conversations

Teachers are used to having all sorts of conversations with their colleagues—from their weekend plans, to their late work policy, to their students who are demanding every last ounce of patience. While many of these conversations involve identifying particular struggles they are having in the classroom, these conversations often don't direct focused attention on improvement. In order for TDO to provide a meaningful learning opportunity for your school, a different kind of conversation about teaching and learning is needed—one that goes beyond identifying needs to discuss specific ideas for improvements. As the principal, you can affect the following key elements for the success of these improvement-oriented conversations: setting the tone, leaving the land of nice, seeing the data, using protocols, and managing roles.

Set the Tone   As the principal, you'll help teachers set the tone of transparency for these conversations. Encouraging lead teachers to be open and transparent about their instruction will affect the degree of value they garner from the TDO process. How can teachers reasonably expect their colleagues to be comfortable sharing data with them about their instruction if they do not set a tone of transparency? Entering into the TDO experience with a learner disposition acknowledges that whether teachers have been in the classroom for ten years or ten months, we are all in a position to improve and refine our practice.

The lead teacher plays a critical role in setting this tone for the conversation. He can focus the group's attention on improvement by asking hard questions about his own practice: "After hearing the data, I wonder how . . . ?" Similarly, he can request feedback and ideas from his colleagues, emphasizing that he is engaged in the process of TDO not just to discuss instruction but to improve it.

As you start the first round of TDO, consider meeting separately with the lead teachers and helping them understand the importance of transparency. You can review with them their focus questions and data collection ideas. If you sense that any of them are holding back, wanting to use TDO as something other than self-improvement such as self-promotion or perhaps simply going through the motions, you can offer feedback that will help them set a more transparent tone with their observers.

The observers can also contribute to a tone of transparency and instructional improvement. They can pose valuable questions, wonderings, and conclusions they draw from the data. The willingness and capacity of even one observer to think hard about the data collected will contribute to the collective value of the experience. Just one substantive question can be the impetus to promote the thinking of the whole group. You can consider using staff meeting time to reinforce the observer role, or perhaps even an e-mail communication or staff memo the day before the first round of observations can be just the reminder that observers need to help set the right tone.

Leave the Land of Nice   It's important to set the right tone for a process focused on improvement. In existing patterns of conversation related to teaching and learning, teachers tend to affirm one another rather than analyze practice. But if they are truly going to improve instruction in their classrooms, they need to engage in conversations that go beyond what's comfortable. For instance, saying, "You did a really great job," is encouraging but does little to inform instructional changes. The land of nice may be a pleasant place to be, but it doesn't cultivate meaningful opportunities for learning. You can encourage teachers to move out of the land of nice by practicing it in your faculty meetings. You can demonstrate that this shift doesn't mean they should abandon respect; rather, it means they should offer their perspective, along with concrete insights, even when those are out of their comfort zone.

In fact, the right tone for TDO is immensely respectful. After all, TDO is about teachers helping other teachers solve important instructional problems. The tone, however, is improvement oriented, and in order to improve, teachers need detailed data and multiple perspectives for interpreting those data and acting on them with new instructional approaches.

> ## Key Point
>
> *If your teachers are going to improve instruction in their classrooms, they need to engage in conversations that go beyond what's comfortable for them. As the principal, you need to set the tone of transparency and focus on instructional improvement for these conversations.*

See the Data Improvement-oriented conversations walk a fine line if they're going to produce the desired results. For instance, if you share data on instruction during faculty meetings but never discuss the implications for improvement, the process is unlikely to yield the instructional insights you seek. You must help teachers in your school learn to regularly ask, "So what?" and then, more important, "Now what?" On the flip side of this, you've got to encourage balance. If teachers make sense of the data or interpret them before sharing the data collectively, they take a similar risk: the observed teacher may not apply comments that are based on data she has not seen. This can make the process feel evaluative, which may inhibit openness to professional learning.

Don't be afraid to call out this balance and the inherent risks in losing track of the balance to your faculty. We have seen many faculties appreciate an acknowledgment from the principals of the potential value and inherent risk of collaboratively analyzing teaching data and helping the lead teacher draw conclusions during a round of TDO.

Use Protocols   So how exactly do you as the principal help teachers find the middle ground between only sharing the data (never climbing the ladder of inference) and jumping straight to conclusions on the data (climbing the ladder of inference too quickly)? In other words, how do you help them climb the ladder of inference intentionally, ensuring that they all see the data before they begin to draw conclusions from what they have seen? The answer is to carefully model the postobservation debriefing protocol. It is developed for this very purpose: to guide the process of making meaning of the data, which are critical improvement-focused conversations. Protocols help teachers climb the ladder of inference intentionally, ensuring that they see all the data collected and draw instructionally relevant conclusions as well.

Manage Roles   Teacher-driven observation conversations require teachers not only to be candid with each another, but to remain humble in the process. Whether they are the observed teacher or the observer, they won't be heard if they are not humble, positioning themselves as a learner no matter what role they take on. We've seen TDO quickly get derailed when one member of the group releases the role of learner and assumes the role of expert. The other participants, whether observer or observed teacher, quickly take a back seat, their expertise and perspective lost from the collaborative setting. If learning were only as simple as having an expert tell us what do to! If it were that easy, we'd all have perfected the art and science of instruction during our teacher preparation programs. There's a reason TDO is collaborative: by nature, it requires multiple perspectives and insights. This value can be culled from TDO only if all participants enter the experience as learners.

Finally, when developing teachers' capacity to engage in improvement-oriented conversations that analyze practice and identify specific changes to better meet student learning needs, it's important to remember that these conversations are about teaching and not about the teacher as an individual. As current and former teachers, we've all had less-than-stellar moments in the classroom, and we're all learning in the process (at least on the good days). This doesn't make us imperfect; it makes us human. If we maintain a focus on improving teaching and learning rather than discussing improving the individual, we'll create a more comfortable space for engaging in meaningful, honest dialogue—the kind of dialogue that is at the heart of TDO.

Build Pedagogical Knowledge

Imagine for a moment that a teacher is examining cooperative grouping in her classroom. In particular, she's interested in collecting data on how students contribute to the thinking of the group. She has observers sit with student groups and script their conversations in order to examine which students are participating and how. As the team makes sense of the data, one teacher notes that effective cooperative learning is built on positive interdependence—a sense that group members need one another to complete a task. When the team discusses this concept in the postobservation meeting, this pedagogical knowledge enriches their conversation. The team builds on this insight by discussing what other evidence of positive interdependence exists in the data and how the lead teacher could cultivate this quality in student groups.

What teachers know affects what they bring to the table as observers. Their knowledge of instructional strategies and effective implementation provides the foundation for gathering and analyzing data in the classroom. Their knowledge informs their development of relevant focus questions and assists them in guiding the observers' attention in the classroom. Without this knowledge as a foundation, they can be shooting in the dark—identifying a strategy that may or may not contribute to student learning. Their attention and energy, though well intentioned, may be misdirected. As a principal, you are uniquely positioned to build schoolwide knowledge of research-based pedagogy that will support teachers as they engage in TDO. Entering the process with this knowledge equips teachers to dig deeper and more thoughtfully into their application of instructional strategies and, in doing so, to meet their students' learning needs most effectively.

As the principal, you have a number of resources you can consult as you lead in building your teachers' reservoir of pedagogical knowledge. We have provided some of our favorites in table 3.1, but that list is just a small sampling of the wealth of resources available. Along with books and printed or online resources, you may choose to employ formal professional development sessions and conferences to develop this knowledge base. You may choose to collaborate with district administrators in this process. Just by reading this book, you're on the right track. What better way to explore the application of pedagogical knowledge in the classroom than through TDO?

In this chapter, we have explored how you can build capacity within your school for teachers to engage in the pre- and postobservation conversations. You can contribute to your teachers' ability to translate data into instructional improvement by improving their pedagogical knowledge through workshops, books, and other sources. Although we were openly critical of traditional professional development in chapter 1 of this book, we have seen workshops on effective pedagogy blossom thanks to the classroom refinement of those practices that TDO offers. TDO will help teachers make the most of those trainings as they apply the concepts in their classrooms and collaborate with their peers in observations. Knowledge of effective pedagogy contributes to robust postobservation debriefing. Teacher-driven observation provides the forum to examine the intersection of the content, students, and instruction. In other words, it deals with the application of knowledge in the classroom.

Key Point

When you invest effort not only in learning the process of TDO but also in building your school's capacity to engage in the process meaningfully, your teachers will gain increased value from the process.

COMMON MISSTEPS

While teachers are the leaders of TDO, school leaders play a critical role in supporting this work in their buildings. As we've discussed in this chapter, there are myriad ways school leaders can build the skills at the core of TDO, support logistics and planning, and cultivate an improvement-oriented environment in which TDO thrives. The missteps we identify here help you further understand your role as a school leader within TDO, ensuring that you're well equipped to support transparent teachers in your building.

Taking the Lead

As a school administrator, you may be most comfortable in positions of formal leadership, and teachers in your school may expect or even wait for you to take the lead. This can be particularly problematic in TDO, a process that positions the observed teacher as leader. When an administrator takes the leadership reins of TDO and directs the focus of the observation, it distorts the purpose: no longer is the primary learning for the lead teacher. Although you have a valuable role to play within TDO in your building, you must remain ever aware that TDO functions by and for teachers. Your role is to support and build their leadership, such that teachers are equipped to identify a focus, facilitate the pre- and postobservation conversations, and create the improvement-oriented culture that is at the heart of TDO.

Neglecting to Leverage Your Leadership

Failing to employ your role as school leader to support TDO efforts can be nearly as problematic as taking too much of a leadership role. Although you are not the leader of TDO, the fact that you are the principal puts you in a unique position to build teachers' capacity and comfort to succeed at it. You can play a critical role in modeling effective facilitation, data-focused and improvement-oriented conversations, and the process of climbing the ladder of inference intentionally. These elements are not specific to TDO. In fact, building teachers' capacities in these areas will benefit all aspects of the improvement work in your building. What better way to embed TDO into the culture of professional learning in your school than infusing the skills of TDO into all staff meetings and conversations? If you hope these skills become part of your school culture, it's critical that you take the lead in modeling them.

Communicating TDO as One More Task

Teachers and school leaders are familiar with the revolving door of initiatives that has unfortunately become characteristic of the profession. It's no wonder that in this environment, TDO can be misperceived as yet another thing on teachers' already full plates. As a school leader, you can play a critical role in messaging TDO. By clarifying what TDO is and what it is not and, more important, illustrating how TDO can support the work teachers are already doing, you'll set up teachers to engage in the process effectively. Create opportunities for teachers to use TDO as a process for more deeply exploring existing initiatives or areas of instructional interest. Tying TDO into these areas can help teachers understand that TDO equips them to do what they are already doing, only better.

FINAL THOUGHTS

Just like the art of teaching itself, TDO requires technical understanding of a process alongside skills that strengthen the implementation of the process. When you invest effort not only learning the process of TDO but also in building your school's capacity to engage in it meaningfully, your teachers will gain increased value from the process. As you embed TDO into professional learning in your school, you'll create the skills within your teams to make it effective. Through your efforts to model the work, linking TDO with professional development, using data, and leveraging collaboration, you will support effective TDO and build your teachers' capacity to engage in meaningful work in all collaborative settings. This one facet alone can have a huge impact on your school because so much of education involves collaborative work. As you support teachers through their planning, facilitation, and improvement-oriented conversations in this skill-building process, your own pedagogical knowledge will increase, and you will generate sustainable results.

The next chapter brings TDO to life using the case study of a large high school that implemented TDO.

CHAPTER EIGHT
TEACHER-DRIVEN OBSERVATION IN ACTION

Having nearly finished this book, you now have clarity about the basics of teacher-driven observation (TDO). At the very least, we hope you are clear on its purpose and potential as a tool for professional growth that leads to improvements in teaching and learning.

In this chapter, we change track. Now that we've presented the TDO process step by step, we'll show you how it looks in practice. This chapter offers a case study describing a comprehensive high school in its third year of implementing TDO (at the time of writing this book). The teachers' experiences in this school show in detail how TDO works.

Hamilton High School in Chandler, Arizona, was an easy choice for the subject of this case study. Hamilton is a massive high school with more faculty members than some of our other partner schools have students. Comprehensive high schools have long been criticized for professional cultures of isolation and privatization among teachers. Therefore, we argue that if Hamilton High School can successfully break down that culture and create a meaningful TDO process, then so can you!

In addition, Hamilton High School approached TDO as an entire school. Much of the model we have presented in this book assumes that TDO will start with an individual teacher who wants to develop professionally. Inviting her peers one by one, a founding teacher can spark an organic movement to schoolwide TDO implementation. At Hamilton, in contrast, the principal instigated TDO, and the process was sustained by department leaders. As you might imagine, it's difficult to successfully implement a teacher-driven professional development process from the top. Hamilton has struck just the right tone.

We, Trent and Emily (the authors), served as professional developers and consultants to Hamilton High in implementing TDO and so use *we* to describe our involvement. Incorporating our part into the following narrative is intended to shed light on how outside expertise may add value to TDO implementation.

After describing the setting a bit more, we walk you through the process from Hamilton's planning phases, all the way through year 2 of its TDO implementation. We show you some of the exciting results the school has seen in the culture of teaching as well as growth in student performance. We end the chapter by looking ahead through the eyes of Hamilton's leaders as they consider how to sustain the work amid dozens of other state- and district-driven initiatives. Hamilton's story is not fully written; it is currently in the middle of its journey. We hope that by discussing the options and ideas that lie ahead for Hamilton, you will begin to consider the future of TDO at your school.

If you are a principal reading this chapter, you'll easily see ways in which Hamilton's tactics can apply to your own school. You'll have the perspective of a whole-school entry point and see what worked for Hamilton's leadership.

If you are a teacher, watch for the teachers' experiences in this case study. Even if your school does not engage in schoolwide implementation, you may still face many situations similar to the teachers in this story. After all, regardless of entry point, TDO unfolds in the classroom, and you're holding the reins.

THE SCHOOL

Nestled in the desert town of Chandler, Arizona, a sprawling suburb of Phoenix, Hamilton High School is a monolith set amid saguaro cactus and residential developments. It's not unusual to see principal Fred DePrez sporting a Hamilton Huskies athletic jacket on any given day or to have him share with you the latest academic and athletic achievements of Hamilton students. Hamilton's reputation for rigorous academics and strong athletics is reflected on the walls and in the display cases in the building. The faces of sports and classroom heroes line the hallways, and the crisp appearance of the building reflects the pride of the community.

Hamilton High serves over 3,500 students and has a teaching faculty of more than 170. Even for the quick-footed, walking from one end of the building to another within the span of the passing bells is a challenge. The sheer size of the building—in space and in numbers—is such that it is not uncommon for teachers to encounter new faces at a faculty meeting or professional development session. While the school's size has undoubtedly contributed to its substantial academic and extracurricular offerings and success, it has also presented unique challenges.

Fred is a visionary who in 2010 determined to transform his school from a traditional American high school into a haven for teacher professional growth, teamwork, and focus on teaching and learning. Fred is also a down-to-earth practitioner who knew he and his team would need to roll up their sleeves and plan for many years of incremental improvements to get to his long-term vision. This chapter represents his team's successful efforts over two years.

PLANNING

In Fred's twelve years as principal of Hamilton High, there had been no lack of professional development for teachers. He recognized that what he hoped to cultivate at the high school was not more professional development but rather more effective professional development that would go beyond hiring more compelling expert speakers or sending teachers to conferences more frequently.

Fred noted that despite the best intentions (his included), current and past professional development efforts were failing to permeate classrooms as deeply as he hoped. For example, although all teachers had gone to training on increasing rigor in their classrooms, their adoption rate for the practices taught at these trainings was very low. He saw teachers enthusiastic about what they had learned as they left the session but who then returned to their regular classroom practices the next day.

In light of this situation, TDO caught his attention at a principals' conference. Fred immediately recognized three ways the model could make a difference at Hamilton. First, he considered how TDO could give his teachers a platform to transfer their learning from the professional development sessions into their classrooms: with TDO, they would be able to try out and perfect the practices with their students that they had learned with their colleagues. Second, he hoped that TDO could reinvigorate his school's professional learning community practice, which had lacked structure. And finally, he saw in TDO the opportunity to get teachers to become transparent in their practice, which would facilitate discussion with one another about teaching.

As Fred pondered implementation, he identified the challenges of rolling out TDO schoolwide. His decades of experience reminded him of the importance of clear communication, particularly with a large faculty. He knew a peer observation model, even a nonevaluative one like TDO, would be a paradigm shift for teachers. Many of them had been observed only for evaluative purposes, so Fred knew he'd have to tread carefully and elucidate the differences between TDO and other observations. Wanting to develop a clear plan for the first full year of implementation and aware of our work supporting school efforts in the district, he enlisted our help in refining and communicating his plan. His goal from the outset was to build the capacity of Hamilton faculty to engage in TDO.

Fred asked us to come to Chandler and meet a team of his teacher leaders and administrators. On a sweltering August day, we met with the team to examine the TDO process in detail and refine a plan for implementing it at Hamilton High. Following an overview of TDO, we role-played in order to offer a solid example of what it encompassed. In this role play, we took the teachers and administrators through each of the steps—a preobservation meeting, an observation (via video), and a postobservation debriefing. At this point, we put our heads together with the teacher leaders and administrators who would be in charge of shepherding this process and sought their suggestions for implementing TDO at Hamilton.

From the outset, the team identified potential sticking points within the model and predicted the type of pushback teachers might give. They hoped this would prepare them for communicating with the staff about TDO. How would teachers identify a focus question? they wondered. Would administrators be involved in TDO? If so, in what capacity? What other resources and support could set teachers up for success? This early meeting set the stage for TDO's success at Hamilton High as this group of teacher leaders identified specific needs and provided suggestions for implementation.

With this team's participation, a full implementation plan for year 1 emerged with these key features:

- *Structure.* Teachers would engage in TDO in four-person, cross-department teams, thereby building collaborative networks outside the existing department structure. In the first year, all teachers would engage in one round of cross-department TDO. The school would provide coverage for one day of release time for all teachers, enabling the team to complete the preobservation conversation during period 1, observations during periods 2 through 5 (one full period of observation per teacher on the team), and the postobservation debriefing during period 6. Table 8.1 illustrates this schedule.

- *Focus.* All teachers had recently read *Never Work Harder Than Your Students*, which would serve as a starting point to develop a focus question.[1] Teachers would identify an area of the book that sparked their interest for improvement and would then be grouped according to this teacher-selected common theme.

- *Administrator role.* Administrators would be involved as observers in each group for each round of observations and would stress their nonevaluative role. Their presence would help teachers gain understanding of the structure in the first round of the process.

- *Training.* The teacher leaders and administrators recognized that implementing TDO well would require focused attention and training, particularly for a school of their size, where messages could easily get misinterpreted in the lines of communication. Therefore, the team decided that we would deliver three two-hour professional development sessions to the entire faculty throughout the coming school year (see figure 8.1). The sessions would serve the purpose of building the required capacity in teachers to engage meaningfully in the process.

TABLE 8.1   HAMILTON HIGH SCHOOL TEACHER-DRIVEN OBSERVATION SCHEDULE

Period 1, 7:25–8:21	Preobservation meetings (all four teachers)
Period 2, 8:26–9:22	Teacher A observation
Period 3, 9:27–10:23	Teacher B observation
Period 4, 10:28–11:41	Teacher C observation
Period 5, 12:17–1:13	Teacher D observation
Period 6, 1:18–2:14	Postobservation debriefing (all four teachers)

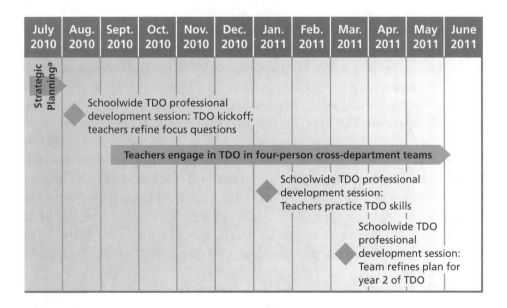

FIGURE 8.1.   Year 1 TDO Implementation Calendar

Note: [a]Teacher leadership team and administrators meet with Education Direction to discuss the TDO process, identify sticking points, and create a plan for communicating it to the staff.

As the Hamilton High team developed the plan, they discussed its objectives for the year. They recognized that many of the TDO practices would be countercultural to some teachers, who rarely had other adults in their classrooms. Thus, the team entered the school year with a singular objective: for all faculty to engage in TDO once in order to build comfort with the process. They knew that these practices would take time to develop, but they were excited about starting implementation.

IMPLEMENTATION: YEAR ONE

Several weeks into the school year, the entire faculty gathered in the cafeteria for the TDO kickoff. Teachers cautiously picked up handouts from a table as they entered the room, wondering what exactly the focus of the day would be. Questioning the value of the meeting, a few carried reading materials and stacks of student work.

The next few hours were full. We introduced the three-part TDO process, explained how it differed from evaluation, and enacted a full role play. During the final portion of the role play, a group of teacher volunteers engaged in a mock postobservation debriefing, sitting in a circle of chairs as their colleagues watched. The volunteers, who had no prior training in TDO, illustrated for their colleagues that any teacher can thoughtfully engage in this work.

Many teachers reported that this fishbowl session was the turning point in their understanding of the process. This setting illuminated the purpose of TDO, particularly as the faculty listened to the observers sharing data using descriptive language and the observed teacher making sense of the data. At the end of the debriefing role play, as the observers handed the lead teacher all of the data they had collected, the teachers could see that TDO was designed to benefit the observed teacher. No doubt remained about the purpose of the process.

Following the role play, teachers worked together in small groups to construct and refine their focus questions. We carefully allotted time for this purpose in order to take advantage of the wealth of ideas available in the collaborative environment. As outside providers, we applied our experience gained from implementing TDO in many schools and brought with us ideas to jump-start the teachers' thinking. At the end of the day, most teachers were ready to dive into TDO with their focus question in hand.

The clock was ticking. Precisely one month later, teams of teachers began the first rounds of TDO at Hamilton High. Teachers completed evaluations of the TDO process following each round of observations, which we collected and shared with the administrative team. These data illustrated that as teachers engaged in TDO, they developed comfort with the process, which demystified it for those in the wings. The positive energy that emerged from these early rounds facilitated future success. Following his first TDO experience, one teacher noted, "This is the best observation experience I've had. It was probably the most beneficial and, at the same time, the most enjoyable."

In January, the faculty came together again—all 170 of them. Over the course of the morning, teachers practiced various skills essential to the TDO process. For instance, they put a variety of observation methods to work as they watched a video of a classroom lesson. They honed their descriptive language as they shared data. The training session focused on more than building teachers' capacity to engage in TDO; the administrative team used it as a forum for collecting feedback. Teachers discussed their feedback in small groups and then submitted it individually in writing, such that the feedback could easily be aggregated across the faculty. Because TDO was designed to benefit teachers, hearing their perspectives was necessary to ensure the process lived up to that objective.

As supporters of the high school's work, we reviewed the feedback and noted specific suggestions teachers provided for improvement. At the final training in March, two months later, we shared a summary of the feedback and refined the TDO plan for year 2. This plan included the following adjustments:

- A structure for interdepartment observations, which would allow teachers to focus more deeply on content and shared content-specific instructional methods.

- An optional change in group size from four to three, thereby enabling teachers to complete a round of observations in a half-day and requiring less time out of the classroom.

- A focus on four specific instructional areas that teachers expressed interest in improving: assessment, student grouping, depth of knowledge, and student participation and engagement.

As we presented these ideas to the teachers at this meeting, we engaged them in a tuning protocol whereby they provided warm and cool feedback to refine the plan for year 2 (see figure 8.2). While this session served as an opportunity to develop the year 2 plan, it was also an occasion to celebrate the accomplishments of year 1. To highlight how far they'd come, we created a slide illustrating the learning of a dozen participating teachers. This slide emphasized the purpose of TDO and its impact on instruction at Hamilton High (see figure 8.3).

Fred and his teams were pleased; they could see the difference TDO made in professional development at their school, even in this first year. The content of this March session emphasized two critical points: TDO is teacher-driven (emphasized through the refinement of the structure and plan for TDO into the future) and instructionally focused.

FIGURE 8.2. Tuning Protocol

This tuning protocol (as in "fine-tune") is a useful tool for allowing a variety of voices and perspectives to be shared, while focusing intently on a specific presentation or plan. The time frame may vary, but adhering to a strict time for each segment is advised.

The process normally takes about forty-five minutes as each team takes a turn going through the following steps. (15 minutes per team)

Introduction

The facilitator briefly introduces protocol goals, norms, and agenda.

Presentation (2 minutes)

The presentation is made by the sharing team and includes the context for material presented, purpose or goal, and sharing samples. No questions are entertained at this time.

Clarifying Questions (2 minutes)

Participants from the feedback teams have an opportunity to ask questions to get information that may have been omitted in the presentation and they think would help them understand the context of the presentation.

Warm Feedback (3 minutes)

Participants from the feedback teams reinforce and call attention to aspects that they think are especially strong and recognize the acknowledgment of problems and issues by the sharing team. This is not about saying, "Good presentation!" It is about being descriptive and helping the presenters see value they might not have seen in their presentation. The sharing team takes notes and does not respond.

Cool (Not Cruel) Feedback (3 minutes)

This is an opportunity for participants from the feedback teams to pose questions that make them wonder, want to know more about, or are confused about. They may also share concerns or raise issues or other ideas that they think are worth exploring. The sharing team takes notes and does not respond yet.

Final Reflection (5 minutes)

This is opportunity for the sharing team members to converse among themselves. The feedback teams listen and do not interact.

Note: For more information, go to the National School Reform Faculty Web site: www.nsrfharmony.org/.

---

ed   **A Snapshot of Instruction**

- I will pay closer attention to how and to whom I redirect my questions.
- I plan on creating some type of system that will help me call on each student during the class.
- I would like to try to let students compare their warm-up answers with each other individually before sharing with the class.
- I was able to see that nonverbal cues had the greatest influence on students' correcting themselves. I will limit the use of the verbal cues and include more modeling and nonverbal cues to evoke corrective behavior by the students.
- Although my students are working on a two-day project, I should end a few minutes early and have some sort of closure activity to solidify the concepts they worked on.
- I want to get some small whiteboards and begin using them to check for comprehension.
- I feel the strategies I will be implementing in the classroom surround the quality over quantity approach, so I will make sure that the actual seat time is the most worthwhile part of the learning process and that homework will not be assigned unless it is a meaningful assignment.
- I will call on more students during a single problem instead of having one student complete the whole problem for us.
- I will work on writing better questions on varying levels of Bloom's taxonomy.
- I need to cultivate the expectation that "I know I will be called on."
- I plan to redirect some student questions to the rest of the class to increase dialogue between students and increase understanding of concepts.
- I plan to assign specific jobs or tasks when students are working in groups to incease accountability.

FIGURE 8.3. A Snapshot of Instruction
Source: Education Direction; Center for Education Reform.

As the first year of implementation wound down and teachers prepared for summer vacation, the administrative team sat around a table in the main office, poring over the evaluation data they had collected on TDO at Hamilton High School. Fred noticed in the data that teachers had developed comfort with opening their classroom doors. He also saw that they valued TDO as a process to promote effective instruction (see figure 8.4). In recognition of their goals at the start of the year, the team deemed the first year of implementation as a learning year.

As Fred and his team reflected on teachers' comments in both formal evaluations of the process and casual conversation, the team recognized that getting

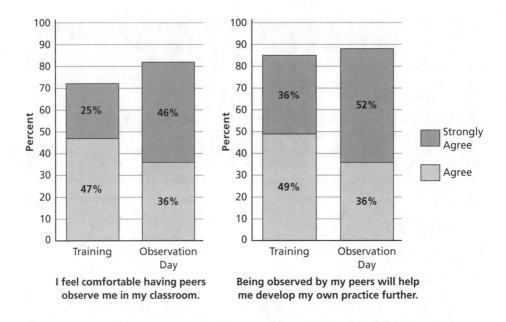

FIGURE 8.4.   Hamilton High School Evaluation Data: Year 1

teachers engaged in the process was the most meaningful way to build their under-standing of TDO. Several teachers had pointed this out: doing the work was the best way to truly understand what TDO is and is not. And when teachers came to under-stand TDO as a nonevaluative practice that responded to needs they identified, their value for the process grew.

Teachers also expressed their appreciation for the chance to contribute to the process, particularly as it informed the second year of implementation. These opportunities—during which the collection of feedback had been not just a superficial exercise but an authentic opportunity to inform the process—had shaped the direction of TDO. Because teachers had directly influenced TDO, the process best met their needs.

As school let out for the summer, Fred's team knew they had a lot of work ahead to prepare for year 2. Over a dozen new teachers would join the faculty next year. The administrative team quantified the resources and support required to transfer the interdepartment observations from idea to practice. Despite the challenges, the team felt optimistic that year 2 would provide an opportunity for them to build on the foundation that teachers had created in year 1.

IMPLEMENTATION: YEAR TWO

As teachers returned for the start of another school year, they gathered in the auditorium to review the TDO process. For a handful of new teachers, this session introduced them to the process. For returning teachers, the training offered an opportunity to think about a focus question and relevant instructional resources. Anticipation was high: teachers were not wondering what the focus would be for this year, but wondering instead how their departments would apply TDO. Their experience from year 1 gave them confidence to engage the process again. Small teams of teachers, grouped by the instructional categories identified at the end of the previous year (assessment, student grouping, depth of knowledge, and student participation and engagement), discussed instructional strategies. As they talked about ways they might leverage TDO to explore the application of these strategies in their classrooms, the auditorium was abuzz with excitement. This positive energy was a definite contrast to the anxiety that had filled the room a year before when teachers were learning about TDO. In only one year, their questions had shifted from, "What will this new process look like for me?" to, "How can I best use this process to improve what I'm doing in my room?"

With a full round of TDO under their belt, teachers entered their next observation free from the nervousness that had been present for many of them during year 1. They were eager for the opportunity to discuss teaching and student learning in the context of their classrooms. They knew what to expect: their peers weren't coming in as evaluators but rather as colleagues who shared a desire to improve teaching and learning in their classrooms.

In year 2, the high school team tailored their objective from simply having all faculty engage in TDO once in order to build comfort with the process to implementing one round of TDO each semester (see figure 8.5). This created two opportunities for every teacher and illustrated the leadership team's year 2 objective: to balance capacity building for TDO with increased flexibility and autonomy for teachers.

Over the course of the first semester, all Hamilton High teachers engaged again in a cross-department observation. As the second semester approached, a new opportunity emerged: administrators gave departments the resources and autonomy to design a TDO model that would best meet their needs. Under the leadership of volunteers, departments allocated professional development time to plan the structure of their observations.

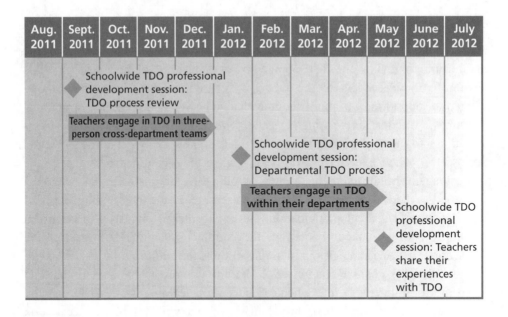

FIGURE 8.5. Year 2 TDO Implementation Calendar

This year 2 shift reflected Fred's goal to hand leadership of TDO increasingly over to teachers. He knew this was the best way to ensure the process would outlast his tenure as principal.

Loosening the structure enabled a new level of innovation to emerge, allowing teachers to tailor TDO more than they'd been able to do in prior rounds. Fred and his team noted that each department took a slightly different approach—one that best met their unique needs. For instance, the fine arts department created a whole-department structure, in which all of its members observed one another over the course of two days. The English department broke up teams by grade level to look at skills particularly relevant to each set of students and their comprehension of nonfiction texts. The math department planned to use partial period observations to explore student engagement. As departments finalized their plans, they submitted these to the administration along with requests for class coverage. The administration responded with support—providing substitutes where requested and giving departments the autonomy they had been promised.

Several months later, as summer vacation approached, we brought teachers together in small groups to share schoolwide data we had collected on their experiences engaging into TDO (see figure 8.6) and explore the successes of the year in order to build into the future. Resoundingly, the teachers expressed the value of

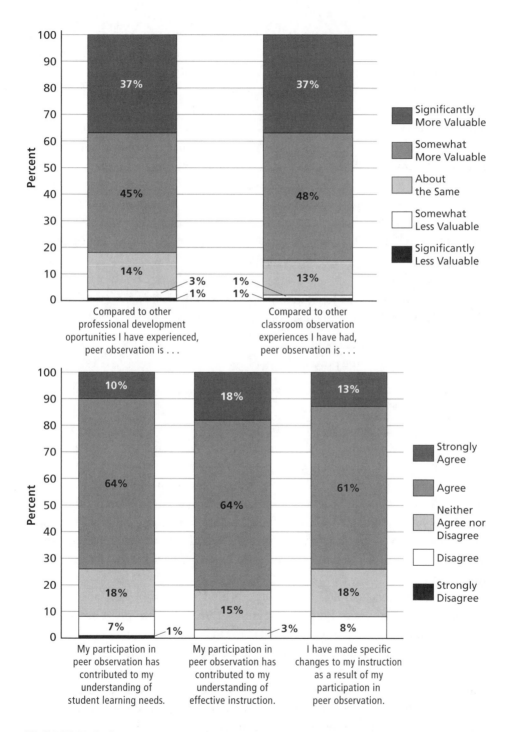

FIGURE 8.6.   Hamilton High School Evaluation Data: Year 2

the department observations alongside the cross-department observations. As the flexibility of the structure increased, so did their learning. However, many cautioned that they had arrived at this point only from first engaging in the work in a structured, whole-school model. As one teacher noted, "The way to learn this work is to engage in this work. In two years, we've really come to a place where we understand what this process truly offers us as teachers."

Teachers discussed the instructional learning they had culled from engagement in TDO. One music teacher said TDO had helped him focus on expanding students' instrument playing time in orchestra. An English teacher shared changes she had made in her classroom to better facilitate student discussions. As teachers described their professional learning, the conversation naturally evolved into identifying the factors that contributed to that learning. Their comments highlighted the value of TDO:

> "I used to think professional development was outside the classroom, but now I know that PD is embedded in the classroom with peers."

> "You can always read about something, but exploring it in the context of the classroom is more powerful."

> "Teachers want to learn. This process recognizes that by providing authentic opportunities for learning."

Hearing these comments, Fred appreciated the success of this particular style of professional development. He saw that as teachers were given the time, support, and autonomy to engage in TDO, the process became their own. Although the idea had stemmed from his vision, teachers were now taking increasing ownership for the process as year 2 concluded. This evolution occurred because he and his team had provided teachers with a structure for doing TDO and simultaneously offered them flexibility (through the department observations) to adapt TDO to their specific needs.

Summer approached, and Fred hung up his Huskies athletics jacket for the season. He sat in his office thinking about how the road to this point had not been without potholes and detours. From the start, his efforts to implement TDO had challenged some teachers' perceptions of classroom observations. Could an observation truly be nonevaluative? That had been a big question during year 1, but by year 2, more important questions had taken center stage. Certainly the logistics of allocating time for a faculty as large as Hamilton's had required a true commitment of resources, and at some level, Fred was amazed that he and his team had pulled it off. It was a testament to their commitment to their faculty, but he knew they'd have made it happen even if they had to provide class coverage themselves. Two years into implementation, TDO had become his school's way of doing business—a proven process for collecting and analyzing classroom data to improve teaching and learning. One teacher noted this: "Rather than focusing on creating a perfect lesson, we're focused on where the kids are at and how we can best support their learning."

LOOKING AHEAD

If two years of TDO was all Hamilton High did, it would be easy to stamp "success" on the project and close the folder. But TDO doesn't regularly finish like that. Rather, TDO became a staple of the professional learning culture at the high school. It encouraged collaboration and dialogue that focused on teaching and learning—a factor that increased the value teachers placed on the process. Following two years of implementation of TDO, over 80 percent of Hamilton High teachers reported that compared with the other professional development and classroom observation experiences in which they had participated, peer observation was more valuable. The same percentage reported that participation in peer observation had contributed to their understanding of effective instruction. Nearly three-quarters reported the process contributed to their understanding of student learning needs. Figure 8.6 summarizes these data.

At this point, Fred's vision is well on its way to fruition: through TDO, the professional culture at Hamilton is shifting. Most important, TDO is contributing to instructional changes in its classrooms. Nearly three-quarters of teachers report making specific instructional changes as a result of their participation, including strategies for increasing student engagement, building students' critical-thinking skills, and better managing their classrooms. Clearly this professional development has had an important impact on the classroom.

The team's enthusiasm about the shifts in professional culture and instruction at Hamilton is equally paralleled by their excitement about improvements in student learning. In 2012, Hamilton High received the highest growth score among Arizona's comprehensive high schools. Further evidence of increased student learning is illustrated in figure 8.7, which shows substantial improvement in all tested areas on the norm-referenced Stanford 10 exam.

Fred and his team have realized that TDO is a means for allowing teachers to help one another become better instructors. At this book's publication, Hamilton has completed two years of TDO and is planning for a third. Hamilton faculty do

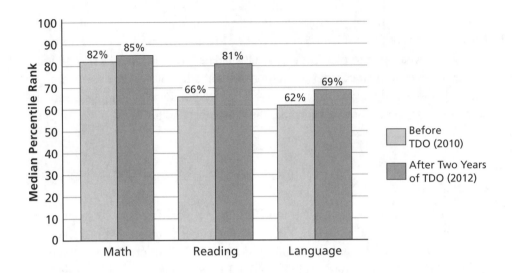

FIGURE 8.7.   Hamilton High Student Results After Two Years of TDO
Implementation.

Source: Arizona Department of Education, School Report Cards:
http://www.ade.az.gov/srcs/find_school.asp

not view TDO as a stand-alone process. As such, they're planning to use TDO in
various focus areas.

First, they appreciate the benefits of giving departments the freedom to deter-
mine how to best leverage TDO within their classrooms. They also foresee loosening
the structure sufficiently that individual teachers can develop their own focus areas
independent of any department or school-level guidance. And in light of a new Arizona state teacher evaluation model, Fred's team plans to use TDO to support the
implementation of this state initiative so that teachers can practice and refine instructional elements embedded in the evaluation model. The new instrument, Marzano's
art and science of teaching framework, includes two domains immediately relevant
to TDO: reflecting on teaching and collegiality and professionalism.[2] What better
way for teachers to engage in "evaluating the effectiveness of specific pedagogical
strategies and behaviors" (element 52) or "promoting positive interactions with colleagues" (element 55) than to engage in classroom-embedded collaborative inquiry
through TDO? Nesting TDO within the Marzano instrument will provide Hamilton
High teachers with an authentic process for meeting the objectives of the model and
illustrate how TDO can support both existing and new initiatives.

Certainly Fred and his team are aware that the field of education evolves; changes always come down the pike. However, they're confident that teacher-driven observation has already become a consistent process for professional learning at Hamilton High School. Through TDO, faculty members are becoming transparent teachers; in doing so, they are taking charge of their learning by exploring their instruction and their students' learning as they open their classroom doors from the inside.

PROFESSIONAL LEARNING COMMUNITIES AND TEACHER-DRIVEN OBSERVATION

As a fourth-grade teacher, Tina appreciated the chance to leave her daily post at the front of the classroom and become a student for the weekend at the education conference. She'd chosen to teach because she was passionate about helping students learn; in fact, that was the goal of the professional learning community (PLC) in her school. When she and her colleagues met once a week, Tina enjoyed the conversation they shared. Topics ranged from general small talk to what they wanted their students to learn in the units they were teaching. Often members of Tina's PLC discussed how to monitor whether students were actually learning those things. Together they'd brainstorm strategies each person could use in the classroom. She was hoping this conference would offer new material she could bring back to her group.

As the first session began on Saturday morning, Tina found a front-row seat and placed her notebook next to her coffee. She watched the presenter enter the room confidently and introduce the topic: "The Transparent Teacher." It was new to her, but it made sense. Weaving together familiar concepts like collaboration, observation, and commitment to learning, TDO encompassed elements that Tina felt were already working well in her PLC.

As the presenter described the process, Tina realized that TDO could help her team effectively collect and analyze data that would inform and improve their teaching. Her team was already good at focusing on what and how well the students were learning, but they didn't regularly focus on what they would do if students didn't learn or if students already knew the material they taught. Even more, they didn't check in with each other to see how their planned interventions worked, or whether one teacher's success might inform another's approach. And certainly, her team members didn't ever watch one another teach.

Tina jotted down insights about how TDO could work for her team. They already had common planning time that they were using for meetings, which they could use for their preobservation meetings. They also had relationships of trust in place so they were well positioned to enter each other's classrooms and gather data. Because they shared students and common unit structures, Tina's team was a built-in group of experts.

As the session ended, Tina was filled with excitement about implementing TDO. While her team regularly talked about things they could do in their teaching, they never actually walked through each other's classrooms doors. Using TDO, they could become transparent teachers, learning what mattered for their students.

Collaboration is not new to teachers, nor is the commitment to enhancing student learning. As consultants to the professionals in the field of education, we interact almost daily with teachers, principals, and administrators who devote their time to making a difference for their students. It's a privilege to see this. We've noticed that teachers regularly pull together through PLCs within schools to enhance their own learning amid their efforts to teach. You may already be a member of a PLC at your school, or you may have heard of them at other schools.

We're often asked how TDO relates to the work of PLCs. Because PLCs have been formed to address such a variety of issues, we'd like to briefly define a typical PLC for the purposes of this epilogue's discussion. That way we'll all be working from a common understanding when we describe the TDO-PLC connection, even if you don't have a PLC or if your PLC looks slightly different.

Dedicated to improving learning in their schools, members of a PLC take action to help students achieve better results. PLCs believe that teachers benefit from continuous learning embedded in their own classrooms. Through collaboration and collective inquiry, PLC teams typically work interdependently to ask and answer critical questions about what the students are learning and what teachers will do to support this learning. Our experience shows that it is easy for teachers to focus on what the students are doing (or should be doing). It's more challenging for them to access and discuss what they themselves are doing (or should be doing).

That's where TDO comes in. We have the privilege of working with groups of enthusiastic teachers who are interested in implementing this sort of observation.

They see the commonalities between TDO and PLCs and often ask us about the relationship. It's a good question. Because the answer is multifaceted, we've structured the remainder of this epilogue to address four common scenarios that define the relationship of TDOs and PLCs (where they exist). Chances are good that one of these scenarios will speak to your own situation:

- How can TDO help us improve our PLC work?

- If we already have a well-functioning PLC, should we do a round of TDO in our PLC, or should we group ourselves differently for TDO?

- If we don't have well-functioning PLCs, could TDO help us improve the functioning of our PLCs?

- If we don't have PLCs, should we create PLCs in conjunction with or as a prerequisite to implementing TDO?

SCENARIO 1: HOW CAN TDO HELP US IMPROVE OUR PLC WORK?

Here a well-functioning PLC team wants to implement TDO to improve their work. TDO can specifically help teams gather data about what teachers can do to support students who may not be learning. Instead of simply discussing questions in a planning meeting, PLC teams can use TDO to gather data. Having data on hand from their own classrooms will help teachers find out if students are learning or if they already know the material. With that information, they can generate specific strategies that address their students' needs.

If your PLC is getting a little stagnant, perhaps spending more time in small talk than in passionate teaching-oriented conversation, TDO can reignite the community. A new process and new data will drive new insights. If your PLC doesn't yet do peer observation (and many don't), TDO can make a big difference. Getting into each other's classrooms opens up transparency; teachers will have a concrete sense for what is really happening and how well it works. From the context of TDO, PLC conversations move to the next level in terms of effectiveness and results.

SCENARIO 2: IF WE ALREADY HAVE A WELL-FUNCTIONING PLC, SHOULD WE DO A ROUND OF TDO IN OUR PLC, OR SHOULD WE GROUP OURSELVES DIFFERENTLY FOR TDO?

The short answer to this question is: it depends. Let's look at pros and cons of both possibilities.

If you stick with your current PLC grouping, you can build on established norms and accumulated trust levels. This is a big advantage; it eliminates a lot of the initial comfort-level legwork that new groups have to cover. However, in terms of observations, this familiarity could go either way: sometimes it's easier to be vulnerable with people you don't know than people you care about impressing. Sometimes it's the other way around. Think for a minute: Are you more invested in what strangers at the grocery store think of your outfit or about what your mother will think of your outfit?

Deciding to build groups outside your established PLC team also carries advantages. While you'll have to establish a level of trust with that group, you'll get to build more connections across your school. This can generate interaction that creates more ideas, more learning, and more growth. Also, consider that forming another group may widen the breadth of what you're able to accomplish. In other words, if you've got a good thing going with your PLC group, why not do something different with your TDO group? Then you can benefit from being part of both groups.

SCENARIO 3: IF WE DON'T HAVE WELL-FUNCTIONING PLCS, COULD TDO HELP US IMPROVE THE FUNCTIONING OF OUR PLCS?

This scenario assumes that you have a PLC, but that it's not as effective as you might wish in its current incarnation. PLCs by nature always have potential, and TDO could be just what your group needs to spring into action.

Part of this answer depends on what elements of your PLC aren't working well. Of the essential characteristics of a PLC, collaboration, collective inquiry, and action orientation are the three areas where TDO can help your team most. If you are struggling with collaboration, TDO sharpens the focus on learning by putting the onus for learning on the teacher who is tackling a problem. While having a learner disposition is essential to both effective TDO and PLCs, TDO is particularly powerful in situating each teacher in the driver's seat of his or her own learning.

If your team is struggling with collective inquiry, TDO is all about leveraging each team member to help with inquiry. Everyone has a role, so the process truly becomes a collective enterprise. When PLC teams aren't experimenting because teachers are unwilling to try new things in the classroom, TDO opens the door to create transparency. You can bet that stagnant teachers will begin to implement new strategies when colleagues are watching. That impetus for active experimentation through TDO will wake up all involved, and you can only guess at the changes that will result.

SCENARIO 4: IF WE DON'T HAVE PLCS, SHOULD WE CREATE PLCS IN CONJUNCTION WITH OR AS A PREREQUISITE TO IMPLEMENTING TDO?

Again, the answer could go both ways. PLCs, especially those that are working well, can be a great vehicle for implementing TDO. There are structures and protocols that the PLC work can teach that we have not presented in this book but that you can use in your TDO process. In that sense, yes, a PLC structure can really propel TDO work.

So is a PLC the way to go with TDO? Not necessarily. The spirit of PLCs is using common planning time to improve teaching and learning. But your school may not have capacity to establish common planning time for you. The good news is that TDO can work in every school every time it is used. It doesn't require common planning time, shared students, or even similar teaching levels. As you've seen in the book, TDO teams can benefit from involving both new and experienced teachers and teachers from different subject areas. It unites teams based on a shared focus on improving learning. Therefore, teams that regularly follow the TDO process will be PLCs in spirit, even if they're not following the letter of the process.

FINAL THOUGHTS

Teacher-driven observation can be the logical next step of PLC work. Like PLCs, TDO embraces collaboration, collective inquiry, and a commitment to job-embedded learning within the classroom. TDO is action oriented and dedicated to improving learning. By providing specific strategies and methods for teachers to take charge and situate professional learning in their classrooms, TDO enables PLC teams to formulate focus questions and gather data. Within this book, you've seen how it creates reliable structure to guide observers in their roles. It situates lead teachers in the driver's seat for their own learning. And it weaves critical inquiry with collaboration in a user-friendly, results-oriented process. It can function within the grouping of PLCs or work effectively with another collaborative teaming structure.

We wish you success as you take charge and implement teacher-driven observation at your school, with your teams, and inside your own classroom.

CHAPTER SUMMARIES AND STUDY QUESTIONS

CHAPTER ONE: TEACHER-DRIVEN OBSERVATION FOR PROFESSIONAL LEARNING

Because one-shot workshops in conference centers and cafeterias are hard pressed to connect with the day-to-day realities of classroom instruction, traditional professional development often falls short of intended outcomes. Professional development is designed to deliver results in a typical school, but each district, school, and classroom has its own defining characteristics. For instance, teacher-student interaction is dynamic, changing minute by minute and person by person. To address this real-time action, professional development needs to deliver commensurately customized and adaptable solutions, and this is generally too tall an order for traditional professional development methods.

Teacher-driven observation (TDO) enables teachers to take charge of their professional learning. It creates a forum for connecting teachers, enabling them to examine what really happens in their classrooms as it is happening. TDO empowers teachers to distill relevant data from dynamic teaching situations in their own classrooms. By opening their classroom doors, becoming transparent in their practice, and moving professional development right into their classrooms and with their students, teachers engage in learning that is immediately relevant. Evolving beyond traditional approaches to professional development, TDO creates a space for practice and refinement that drives meaningful instructional improvements.

Questions

1. What is your experience with professional development? Describe a situation where it has made a lasting impact in your classroom.

2. Can you think of a professional development session you've attended that has failed to meet the needs of your classroom? How might you have restructured it if you'd been in charge?

3. What types of professional development are most relevant to you? What themes are you interested in? What topics might enhance your unique teaching style? Name a few.

4. How would you describe the professional culture in your school? In what ways is your school already prepared for the TDO process? What elements would you need to intentionally prepare if you and your colleagues were to implement TDO?

5. Describe what it means for you to become a transparent teacher. In what ways would it make a lasting difference for you to open up your practice and move professional development from the convention center (or cafeteria) into your classroom?

CHAPTER TWO: PREPARING FOR TEACHER-DRIVEN OBSERVATION

Within the structure of TDO, you have ample opportunity to take charge and tailor it to your classroom's particular needs. Teacher-driven observation represents an opening of classroom doors from the inside, not the outside. This fundamental shift empowers observed teachers to establish the goals for the observation. This observation is about gathering data for improvement, not for accountability or evaluation. It is grounded in formative, not summative, data.

Teacher-driven observation is not designed for drawing conclusions about the quality of a teacher's instruction; rather, it focuses on collecting actionable, real-time classroom data that equip teachers to make instructional improvements. It situates professional learning in the classroom. Using scripting, counting, or tracking methods, observers gather data requested by the lead teacher. Any observing teacher, new or veteran, who sincerely seeks to answer the lead teacher's questions can add meaningful value. Throughout its three steps—the preobservation meeting, the observation itself, and the postobservation debriefing—the lead teacher, observers, and administrators work in specific roles. Enabling teachers to do better what they're already doing, TDO is not an add-on or stand-alone practice; it becomes embedded in teachers' work.

Questions

1. How is TDO different in purpose and process from other types of observations that occur in a school? You might construct your answer to this question in terms of what TDO is and is not.

2. What does it mean for teachers to open classroom doors from the inside? Why is this metaphor so important to understanding the purpose of TDO?

3. In what ways are all teachers qualified to participate as TDO observers?

4. When you are an observing teacher in the TDO process, what mind-set can you cultivate to best fulfill your role as a data gatherer?

5. Why do you believe the authors place such a strong emphasis on data collection? As you discuss this question, you might consider how a data-based observation occurs differently from an evaluation-based observation.

CHAPTER THREE: THE PREOBSERVATION MEETING

Successful TDO starts with the preobservation meeting. As the lead teacher, you are in charge of preparing for this meeting by identifying a persistent issue you're struggling with or that you want to know more about. This issue will become the basis for developing your focus question, which will help you examine the connection between your instruction and student learning. Your focus question both informs and drives the entire observation process. Depending on your focus, you'll select specific data collection methods for your observers to use. The most common methods are counting, tracking, and scripting, but you can tailor them to your specific setting.

Your focus question also plays a role in determining who will collect the data. You could recruit observers from a range of experience levels and perspectives to help you see things in your classroom and in the data that you wouldn't discern on your own. Or you might invite observers who have similar backgrounds to your own in order to help you examine the details more deeply. As the lead teacher, you'll also be responsible for ironing out the logistics involved with the observation and its pre- and postobservation meetings.

In a world of virtual private practice, opening your classroom door involves much more than having other teachers sit in your classroom as you teach your students. Success demands thought and preparation, a process that begins long before you find yourself teaching a lesson as your peers observe and collect data. The preobservation meeting is the first step in creating professional development inside your classroom.

Questions

1. Thinking about your own classroom, identify a few questions you have about how you can improve student learning. Which of these questions seems most

pressing for you now? What kind of information would you need to gather in order to answer this question?

2. What are some possible data collection methods that could lend themselves to answering your focus questions? Prioritize your list by identifying which methods you believe are most relevant to your focus questions. If you're stumped, consider how counting, tracking, and scripting could gather data to answer your focus questions.

3. What are common missteps you should keep in mind as you prepare to lead effective preobservation meetings? You could discuss the suggestions at the end of the chapter or offer your own based on your experience.

4. How could approaching TDO as a "model classroom" observation process prevent you from getting the data you need to generate answers to your focus question?

CHAPTER FOUR: THE OBSERVATION

When we open our doors and invite our colleagues in to collect data, we replace isolation with connection and take charge of our professional development. When we're teaching, we don't have extra eyes to examine what's going on in the classroom. We're busy making connections, asking questions, and delivering content, so we don't consciously notice how many students asked questions or how our movements in the room affected student participation. Fortunately, our colleagues can put their eyes, ears, and experience to work for us right in our classrooms. When they step in to observe, we benefit from their capacity to collect data that demonstrate what's happening with our students right now.

Observers use scripting, counting, and tracking methodologies to gather data from teachers and students. In scripting, the observer describes interaction among students and between students and the teacher. Counting data reveals the distribution of classroom time, the percentage of students on task, or the number of questions a teacher asks from each level of Bloom's taxonomy. Tracking data collection methods illustrate patterns of student and teacher movement, nonverbal cues, and eye contact during a lesson. Working simultaneously, observers can use each of these methods to assemble data that create a multidimensional image of classroom activity. Observers must remember to focus only on data collection rather than on drawing conclusions.

What occurs in the classroom powerfully illustrates the intersection of student, teacher, and content. As we stand in each other's classrooms, we can watch how these three elements of the instructional core interact with each other and how those interactions affect teaching and learning.

Questions

1. Imagine that you are the lead teacher. What could you do to reduce any anxiety that you feel about having observers in your classroom? How could you put your observers at ease?

2. What can you do to prepare students for having observers in your classroom? How might the way you explain the observation with your students influence the quality of data that your observers collect?

3. Under what circumstances would you consider having observers interact with students during a TDO observation?

4. As an observer, what might you do to reduce the anxiety that the lead teacher may feel about having you in her classroom? How might making meaning of data rather than simply collecting data affect the outcome of the observation?

CHAPTER FIVE: THE POSTOBSERVATION DEBRIEFING

The postobservation debriefing provides the structure for observers and lead teachers to put their heads together and collaboratively generate insights. Discussing the data is part of this debriefing. The objective of TDO is to inform and guide improvements in teaching and learning—specifically in the area of the lead teacher's focus question. To that end, it's critical for the lead teacher to take charge and guide the meeting. The debriefing is an opportunity not only to discuss the data collected but also to commit to next steps.

The protocol starts as the observers share their data descriptively and briefly. Then the observed teacher reflects aloud about how the data relate to her area for development and illuminate her focus question. It concludes as the group discusses how the data will inform future instruction. Here they may describe future focus areas or new strategies they'll implement. Each of these elements—sharing data, teacher reflection, and next steps—has a specific discussion time allotted to it.

A successful debriefing will make or break the entire TDO process because it memorializes the professional growth and learning. You can ensure the effectiveness of postobservation debriefing by strictly following the sequence of the protocol, using your time effectively, and staying focused on the data.

Questions

1. Why do you believe the authors give special attention to the value of using protocols? How might the use of protocols (a) set TDO up for success at your school and (b) improve other collaborative processes at your school?

2. Why do you think time allotments are important in the postobservation debriefing? How could ignoring the sequence and time allocation in the protocol undermine its success?

3. As you consider the debriefing protocol, which parts of the conversation seem most challenging to you? Can you see already which might be the hardest for you and a team of colleagues to replicate? What preparations can you make to move toward that level of conversation at your school?

4. What biases might you have as an observer in TDO? How might these show up as problematic, especially in your role during the debriefing? Can you think of a strategy for leaving your biases at the door?

5. In the land of nice, everyone stays on safe ground and doesn't challenge anyone else. How could focusing your insights on teaching and practice rather than on the people involved help you exit the land of nice?

CHAPTER SIX: FIGURING OUT THE LOGISTICS

This chapter highlights three key entry points for the TDO process: an individual teacher, a group of teachers, or an entire faculty. Each offers its own unique benefits. You take charge of your professional learning by deciding which entry point suits your specific circumstances best.

The individual entry point—a single teacher engages others in one observation—puts the greatest amount of responsibility on the lead teacher and simultaneously provides the greatest level of autonomy. The timing of and learning from the observation are authentically grounded in the lead teacher's own interest. Alternatively, teacher teams provide both a convenient entry point and a context for an ongoing TDO process, where teachers can revisit a student need or strategy over the course of time or each team member can lead the process a few times throughout a school year. Having a consistent team allows teachers to dig deeply into a topic and its implications for instruction. The teams can form within departments or grade levels, professional learning communities, or even groups of teachers who eat lunch together.

Having a shared and open practice becomes the way of doing business among a faculty when an administrator chooses the entire school as the TDO entry point.

The schoolwide model is an extension of the team model, as it involves several teacher teams engaged in TDO and implies schoolwide participation over a period of weeks or months. It creates collective momentum toward breaking down the professional isolation that's common in many buildings. TDO doesn't need to be resource intensive: you can find creative ways to use scarce resources such as time (with common planning time, before and after school time, and lunch time), personnel (with administrators, educational support staff, and substitute teachers), and funding (with professional development funds and shared substitute teachers).

Questions

1. As you consider your school's circumstances today, which entry point seems most appropriate? How might you communicate this strategy to motivate those you'd like to involve?

2. What advantages and what challenges can you foresee in the process of initiating TDO at the individual level? What about at the team level?

3. What strategies have proven particularly useful when your school has successfully implemented programs schoolwide? How could these strategies help schoolwide TDO implementation go smoothly?

4. In terms of resources, how could you leverage available time, personnel, and funding when implementing TDO at your school? Along these lines, you might consider how you could use administrators, peers, support staff, or substitute teachers in your first round of TDO.

CHAPTER SEVEN: FOR PRINCIPALS: HOW TO IMPLEMENT AND SUSTAIN TEACHER-DRIVEN OBSERVATION

It is important for you as a principal to communicate with teachers that TDO is about improvement, not evaluation. Persistence in this line of communication, especially coming from you, will help defuse anxiety about TDO. Another smart move as a principal is to integrate TDO with other improvement efforts. This signals to teachers that TDO will help them do what they are currently doing better instead of being something new on their already-full plates.

As you begin the process, be intentional about fertilizing the early TDO seeds that you plant because the first fruits of your labors will be your best asset as you look to increase and improve adoption. While your first steps are important, you can also signal transparency to your staff by listening to early feedback and implementing suggested adaptations. Teacher-driven observation is not a one-size-fits-all approach or a silver bullet. As you work to build capacity throughout your building and refine TDO for your school, your teachers will take charge of their professional learning and students will benefit.

EPILOGUE: PROFESSIONAL LEARNING COMMUNITIES AND TEACHER-DRIVEN OBSERVATION

Dedicated to improving learning in their schools, members of a professional learning community (PLC) take action to help students achieve better results. These communities believe that teachers benefit from continuous learning embedded in their own classrooms. Through collaboration and collective inquiry, PLC teams typically work interdependently to ask and answer critical questions about what and how students learn and how teachers will support students who are not learning or already know the material.

By providing specific strategies and methods, TDO enables PLC teams to formulate focus questions and gather data about what the teachers need to do. Teacher-driven observation provides a reliable structure to guide observers in their roles, and it situates lead teachers in the driver's seat, taking charge of their own learning. Building on the work of PLCs, TDO weaves critical inquiry with collaboration in a user-friendly, results-oriented process. It can function within the grouping of PLCs, or it can work effectively outside PLC structure. TDO can jump-start stagnant PLC groups and increase transparency. TDO also creates space for non-PLC teachers to collaborate across a school and implement effective strategies.

Questions

1. What are some advantages that well-functioning PLCs might have in doing a round of TDO within their established PLC groups?

2. In schools that have PLCs, what benefits could teachers gain from working with TDO groups outside their PLC teams?

3. If you don't already have PLCs at your school, should you create them in conjunction with, or as a prerequisite to, implementing TDO? What advantages can you think of related to doing TDO independent from any PLC?

NOTES

Chapter One

1. National Commission on Teaching and America's Future, *What matters most: teaching for America's future* (New York: National Commission on Teaching and America's Future, 1996); A. Lowrey, "Big Study Links Good Teachers to Lasting Gain," *New York Times*, January 6, 2012; L. Darling-Hammond, "Teacher Quality and Student Achievement: A Review of State Policy Evidence," *Education Policy Analysis Archives* 8 (2000): 1–44.
2. C. J. Casteel and K. G. Ballantyne, eds., *Professional Development in Action: Improving Teaching for English Learners* (Washington, DC: National Clearinghouse for English Language Acquisition, 2010), http://www.ncela.gwu.edu/files/uploads/3/PD^in^Action.pdf.
3. T. Wagner, "Leadership for Learning: An Action Theory of School Change," *Phi Delta Kappan* 82 (2001): 378–383.
4. Casteel and Ballantyne, *Professional Development in Action*, 21.
5. D. L. Ball and D. K. Cohen, "Developing Practice, Developing Practitioners: Toward a Practice-Based Theory of Professional Education," in G. Sykes and L. Darling-Hammond, eds., *Teaching as the Learning Profession: Handbook of Policy and Practice* (San Francisco: Jossey-Bass, 1999), 10.
6. R. Elmore, *Bridging the Gap Between Standards and Achievement: The Imperative for Professional Development in Education* (Washington, DC: Albert Shanker Institute, 2002), 29–30.
7. N. Claire, "Teacher Study Groups: Persistent Questions and Promising Approach," *TESOL Quarterly* 32 (1998): 466.
8. R. Elmore, *School Reform from the Inside Out* (Cambridge, MA: Harvard University Press, 2002), 127.
9. K. A. Ericsson, R. T. Krampe, and T. Clemens, "The Role of Deliberate Practice in the Acquisition of Expert Performance," *Psychological Review* 100 (1993): 368.
10. Ball and Cohen, "Developing Practice, Developing Practitioners," 19.
11. R. DuFour, R. DuFour, R. Eaker, and T. Many, *Learning by Doing: A Handbook for Professional Learning Communities at Work* (Bloomington, IN: Solution Tree, 2006), 3.

Chapter Two

1. M. O. Richardson, "Peer Observation: Learning from One Another," *NEA Higher Education Journal* 16:1 (2000), 9–20.

Chapter Four

1. D. L. Ball and D. Cohen, "Developing Practice, Developing Practitioners: Toward a Practice-Based Theory of Professional Education," in G. Sykes and L. Darling-Hammond, eds., *Teaching as the Learning Profession: Handbook of Policy and Practice,* (San Francisco: Jossey-Bass, 1999),

3–32. Richard Elmore has discussed the instructional core in multiple publications including *Instructional Rounds in Education: A Network Approach to Improving Teaching and Learning* coauthored with E. City, S. Fiarman, and L. Teitel (Cambridge, MA: Harvard Education Press, 2009).

Chapter Five

1. J. McDonald, N. Mohr, A. Dichter, and E. McDonald, *The Power of Protocols* (New York: Teachers College Press, 2007), 7.
2. C. Argyris, *Overcoming Organizational Defenses: Facilitating Organizational Learning* (Boston: Allyn and Bacon, 1990).
3. E. City, R. Elmore, E. Fiarman, and L. Teitel, *Instructional Rounds in Education: A Network Approach to Improving Teaching and Learning* (Cambridge, MA: Harvard Education Press, 2009).
4. McDonald et al., *The Power of Protocols.*
5. City et al., *Instructional Rounds in Education.*

Chapter Seven

1. R.J. Marzano, T. Frontier, and D. Livingston, *Effective Supervision: Supporting the Art and Science of Teaching* (Alexandria, VA: Association for Supervision and Curriculum Development, 2011).

Chapter Eight

1. R. Jackson, *Never Work Harder Than Your Students* (Alexandria, VA: Association for Supervision and Curriculum Development, 2009).
2. R. J. Marzano, T. Frontier, and D. Livingston, *Effective Supervision: Supporting the Art and Science of Teaching* (Alexandria, VA: Association for Supervision and Curriculum Development, 2011).

Index